THE WOVEN WORD

"Combining ritual and the sacred with the everyday world. Romany in this timeless work will bridge the gap that once did not exist between the spiritual and actual. Wander into the world of beauty and wonder in these pages and return to a reality tinged with rainbow magick. We will return to this book many times and at different life stages but it will always retain the freshness and inspiration of the first journey."

Cassandra Eason, author of *The Magick of Faeries, The New Crystal Bible,* and *A Year and a Day in Magick*

"A fascinating book celebrating and utilizing the power of the word both spoken and written with all areas of the Craft, inclu~~ding beautiful prose blessings meditations visualizations~~ and i⸻⸻⸻⸻⸻⸻ the great⸻ Rach⸻

⸻gic

"Romany Rivers has created a valuable compendium of poetic verse, ready and waiting for use in your favorite ritual. I wish she had written this book years ago – it would have saved me hours of slogging through piles of poetry and ritual books, searching for the words that would move the participants at the rituals I officiated. Thankfully, it is available now, providing the grateful reader with a wide variety of lyrical verse for use from the opening of the ritual through to the close. Ms. Rivers has thoughtfully included full sample rituals that demonstrate the effective use of her beautiful verse, as well as an extensive set of

correspondences that will provide inspiration for the creation of rituals uniquely suited to each occasion."
Laura Perry, author of *Ariadne's Thread: Awakening the Wonders of the Ancient Minoans in Our Modern Lives*

"In *The Woven Word* Romany has created a real treasure that is destined to become a reference book for everyone interested in learning or developing their own rituals, invocations and practice. There is something here for every occasion and all of it easily adapted to fit the needs of any solitary practitioner or group no matter what their level of experience. Words have power and this comes over very clearly in this careful and considered compendium based on Romany's own experience as a High Priestess and clear love of ritual and her craft."
Yvonne Ryves, author of *Shaman Pathways Web of Life*

"I love, love, love *The Woven Word*! I adore its simplicity, the way that it feels so old and yet so fresh at the same time. There is an akashic nature to what Romany has written here, this book almost feels channeled straight from the Divine."
Arietta Bryant, author of *Ramblings and Rhymes and Circles of Sacred Laughter*

The Woven Word

A Book of Invocations
and Inspirations

The Woven Word

A Book of Invocations and Inspirations

Romany Rivers

Winchester, UK
Washington, USA

First published by Moon Books, 2014
Moon Books is an imprint of John Hunt Publishing Ltd., Laurel House, Station Approach,
Alresford, Hants, SO24 9JH, UK
office1@jhpbooks.net
www.johnhuntpublishing.com
www.moon-books.net

For distributor details and how to order please visit the 'Ordering' section on our website.

Text copyright: Romany Rivers 2013

ISBN: 978 1 78279 542 1

A CIP catalogue record for this book is available from the British Library.

Design: Stuart Davies
www.stuartdaviesart.com

Printed in the USA by Edwards Brothers Malloy

We operate a distinctive and ethical publishing philosophy in all
areas of our business, from our global network of authors to
production and worldwide distribution.

CONTENTS

Acknowledgements

This book is dedicated to just a few of the wonderful teachers and mentors I have had in my life, to whom I am truly grateful. With their time and support, I have learned to trust myself, to know myself, to deeper understand my connection with the world around me.

To my spiritual sister Arietta, who showed me what it meant to be a Priestess within the community, and supported me every step of the way as I balanced my solitary nature with community action. Even now, thousands of miles between us, I still feel your hand on my shoulder in times of need.

To Cassandra Eason, whose constant support and guidance pushed me to put pen to paper, and showed me that a Witch is not what you do, but who you are.

To Ingrid Hart, who blessed me with training in Reiki and so much more. Your gentle energy and broad perspectives opened and healed old wounds, teaching me to face my shadows and shine a light into the darkest corners of my psyche.

Foreword

Sacred Sounds

In one of the major creation myths of Ancient Egypt the God Ptah thought the world in his mind and then created it by speaking magickal words or hekau. The power he used was called heka, which represents as well as the God of that name, the lifeforce. This power animates everything as it did at the first creation. In some versions of the myth, it was the God Heka himself who spoke creation into being. So to the Ancient Egyptians, every act of magick was a recreation of that first act of creation. From Ancient Greek times, harmonious sounds have been regarded as a microcosm or earthly expression of the harmony of the heavenly bodies. Since only a small proportion of the vibrations of the universe could be heard by the human ear, the purpose of chant and song was to attune the spirit of the chanter or musician to these more subtle spiritual sounds on higher levels. In doing so, the soul might move closer to harmony and unity with the cosmic rhythms. Through this attunement, the disparate elements and energies of a spell are harmonized and raised to create the spiritual state and substance of aether, spirit or akasha. In this magickal state or energy force, our wishes are held beyond measured time, filled with power, transformed and bounced back into actuality.

Chanting, the art of saying or singing repetitive words or phrases rhythmically, has been used magickally and in religious and mystical ceremonies for thousands of years. Chanting involves a special thought mode, not just the logical left brain analyzing and categorizing in words, our conscious thoughts. Nor is it quite like the right brain clairvoyance or enhanced visualization, where we work primarily through images. Chanting at its most powerful synthesizes left and right brain to evoke a spiritual out-of-body state that may seem to last for an hour or more, though the chant may only be for five minutes. Chants have the effect of organizing words into a natural rhythm, compressing spell wishes into magickal rather than everyday language structures and so concentrating concepts. In this way, their meaning is powerfully impressed on the aether created by the spell and on our auras, which are likewise empowered by the repetitive and often increasing intensity of the sounds. Whether using voice alone or accompanied by dancing and / or drumming, in isolation or with others, chanting increases the spell tempo and is the single most effective way of raising and releasing power. It also positively affects the chakras, the psychic energy centers and the aura of the chanter. What is more, when chanting is a part of a ritual in which other voices are joined, great collective spiritual and psychic power is generated to launch a need, healing, blessing or empowerment.

In contrast, soft chanting will soothe and harmonize the spirit, creating a light trance in the chanter (and any listeners). This is excellent for becoming receptive to channeled wisdom, for healing spells, empowering herbs or charm bags, and for creating personal harmony and stillness. Mantras that originate in the Hindu and Buddhist traditions involve chanting sacred words or phrases aloud or in the mind. Mantras can be perfected by adepts as a means of developing and channeling psychic energies whether for healing, for positive power, or astral, out-of-body travel.

These concepts have entered modern magick down the millennia and many Witches know from experience that by using words powerfully and wisely, thoughts and desires can be brought into actuality through spells, invocations and ritual prayers. In magick, all words spoken in ritual or as part of a spell are intrinsically powerful and therefore it is important in devising ritual to use words wisely.

Cassandra Eason

Introduction

This book is for students and teachers, those with much to learn, those who have learned much and those who have forgotten more than they have remembered. It is for solitaries and for groups. It for quick reference, for slow perusal, for use and for adaptation. It is designed to be spoken aloud in theatrical representation, or spoken softly in quiet meditation. It is designed to invoke Divine thought as well as the Divine Spirit.

This book has been a labor of love and a spiritual journey for me. I have spent much time and energy connecting with the spirit around us to collate the inspirations listed here. It has been an incredible learning experience for me to connect with deities that I do not often work with in order to create a lyrical call that matches their individual essences. This book has taken many years of work, and many months of sitting unattended and ignored on my laptop when life seemed to take more precedence. In fits and starts I would focus and make the effort to reconnect with words already written and blank pages yet to be filled. Slowly it took shape, changed shape and became something different from my original expectations. I struggled to birth this Frankenstein's creature of ideas and eventually, as with all births, I surrendered to the process, stepped back and watched its graceful and healing transformation into the book that you hold in your hands.

I hope that each and every one of you finds something special within its pages. I hope that it inspires, uplifts, encourages and assists you in your own spiritual journey. I hope that the words on the pages find freedom on the winds of your breath, that they soar into the air, echo over hills and mountain tops, forest and glade. I hope they sink blissfully into the furnishings of your surroundings, absorb into your ritual space with comfort and ease. I hope that they offer blessings to you and your kin in times of hardship and difficulty, in times of joy and celebration. I hope above all else that they find a home in your heart, a thought in your mind, and a voice on your tongue. To feel, connect with and speak the written word is to give life to thought. May these words live on in you.

Romany Rivers

The Essence of Ritual

It's experiential. A profoundly personal act even when shared, ritual reconditions our perspective. It is the practice of reminding ourselves of the value and power of living. It is that moment in which we stop and, looking around, understand that life is sacred.
– Emma Restall Orr, *Ritual – A Guide to Love, Life and Inspiration*

There is an abundance of books and resources available in this day and age that can share the step-by-step process of ritual. We are told where to stand, what actions to take, when to speak, when to be silent. With the greatest will in the world, without the experiential essence of ritual, these words remain words. The actions remain actions. The silence remains silence. This book you hold in your hands is filled with such words, hundreds of words, thousands of words, and the combination of these words holds power. Each sound, each word, each phrase holds power. Yet they do not hold THE power. Without you and your conscious energetic connection to the Divine they remain vibrant, inspiring, thought provoking, energetic, but devoid of Divinity, unable to manifest change beyond their natural environmental impact. You are the power. You are part of the Divine, of the all that is, of the all that was, of the all that will be. You are the essence of ritual.

Ritual comes in three main forms, celebrations of nature, magical rites, and rites of passage. Celebrations of nature include the traditional Sabbats that mark the passage of the Wheel of the Year, as well as any celebration of the Divine within seasonal cycles, planting and harvesting blessings, and communing with nature's deep mysteries. Since Witches see the Divine as immanent within nature, such celebrations allow for a glimpse of the Gods as they manifest within our world and offer a chance to connect with the Gods' energetic journeys so visibly reflected within the seasons.

Magical rites are usually held to coincide with lunar phases, and involve a deep connection with the power of consciousness, the energetic systems of the universe, Divine and spiritual powers. Most often these rites are used to manifest positive change and healing, although magical rites can and do cover a wide range of subjects.

Rites of passage are very important in most Pagan paths and cover a wide range of acknowledgements for life transitions and milestones. Hatches, matches and dispatches – Baby Blessings, Marriages and Funerals – are most commonly understood as rites of passage, but many other transitions are marked within the Witchcraft community, including traditional initiation ceremonies, spiritual transitions and life transitions from one phase to another, such as maiden to mother and mother to crone.

Pagans as a rule are very creative, and many rituals and celebrations are formed by weaving these threads together. For many, any ritual act is a magical act, any celebration of life transition is also a celebration of seasonal cycles, any celebration of nature is also a celebration of the Divine in many forms, and any connection with the Divine is a magical act.

How does one describe not the steps, actions and words of ritual, but that almost intangible connection that separates theater and performance from the sacred play? It is as unique as each practitioner. I stand solitary in my home-based ritual room, surrounded by the objects of my creativity and learning. I stand in the loosely formed circle of my peers, still buzzing and chatting prior to the night's rite. I stand under the moon and gaze up at her impassive face as the breeze chills and thrills my warm skin. I stand. I breathe in. I breathe out. I breathe in deeply. I breathe out the day's stress, and worry, and anxieties. I breathe in the stillness. And then, I can feel it. The otherworldly sensation of falling away, falling out of myself, out of the world, out of time, out of space and yet feeling more rooted into my own body and spirit, deeply rooted in the earth beneath me, rooted into the web of connectivity. I relax into it. I revel in the deep abundant well of joy I can feel. The mundane slips away, yet also falls into sharp relief for all that it is. I accept it all and then let it go. In this space that is no place, and at this time outside of linear time, I simply am who I am. And who I am is Divine.

To me, this is the true essence of ritual. The pure undiluted connection to all that is sacred. The understanding of Divinity and our own Divine spirit. The ability to consciously connect and affect the web of energy around us and within us. The words we speak, the techniques we employ, the practices we use are all powerful in their own way, but this deep-rooted connection is what gives our rituals true meaning. Some of the words within these pages are designed to help affirm that connection, to wake up our own sleepy spirits, and to access the energy all around us. Some of these words need that connection with Divine energy to give them life and meaning. Only you can know what works for you as a spiritual practitioner. I humbly offer my own experiences and inspirations to you, and by doing so I extend my connection to the earth beneath my feet and to my kith and kin who honor her.

Weaving Words of Power

To bind the spell every time
Let the spell be spoke in rhyme
– The Wiccan Rede

The use of language in ritual is an often undervalued or misunderstood technique. Much attention is placed upon intention and Will, without which our magic fails to be effective or affective. Energy follows thought, and as such we focus on refining, honing and harnessing our thoughts, threading our thoughts with clear intention and strength of Will.

Mahatma Gandhi said, "Carefully watch your thoughts, for they become your words. Manage and watch your words, for they will become your actions."

Words become thought, and thought becomes word, the two are interlinked and both greatly impact our actions. When we disregard the importance of verbal or written language within ritual, we do a great disservice to ourselves and to the Divine. Spoken language is not just a method of communicating our intention, desires or Will, it is by its very nature an *energetic technique*. "When your mother told you, "It is not what you said, it is how you said it", she was tapping into the importance of tone, key, inflection, and energetic influence of your speech.

Words can hurt or heal, and the way we communicate with others can shape our present and future relationships. It is a lesson we learn as children, and a lesson that many practitioners are relearning on their magical path. Adding depth to the idea of tone and inflection, we can also observe how each individual syllable is a distinct sound and the combination of sounds within a sentence creates a unique energetic signature. Spoken language is, at its core, sound vibration. These vibrations carry energetic influence into the world around us. When we are conscious not only of what we say, but how we say it, we add to our magic by creating a deliberate weaving of energy expressed through sound. We create words of power.

From the Hermetic philosophers who taught that one of the seven principles of the universe is vibration, "Nothing rests; everything moves; everything vibrates"; to Buddhist teachings of sound, prayers and mantras creating both internal and external effects; and all the way to modern principles of string theory, we can see the potential impact of spoken language. When language is broken into its simplest interpretation of pure sound, the greatest minds all point to the deep mystery of energetic and physical effect created by the unique vibration of sound. The complexities we add to this root vibration by combining sounds and attributing meaning to every combination, gives us the beauty and magic of language.

Sound Influencing Matter

Dr. Hans Jenny, a Swiss medical doctor and scientist, completed some fascinating experiments on the study of wave phenomena, which he called Cymatics (from the Greek *Kyma,* meaning "wave"). The importance and influence of vibration and sound on physical matter can be clearly seen in these simple and elegant experiments. In the 1960s Dr. Jenny placed sand, fluid and powders on metal plates which were then vibrated with a frequency generator and speaker. Different frequencies produced beautiful and often intricate geometric images and patterns that were unique to each individual vibration. When the sound vibration stopped pulsing through the substance, the images collapsed back into their original state. For many practitioners of magic and for practitioners of science, these experiments show that there is a clear impact of sound on matter, that different frequencies produce different results, that sound can alter form, that sound can maintain form, and that sound can create form.

The Written Word Influencing Matter

Dr. Masaru Emoto is well known for his experimentation with water crystals, and his book series *Messages from Water* are filled with stunning images of water crystals affected by sound vibration, spoken word and positive prayer. Dr. Emoto carried the concept of sound vibration further, by looking at the energy of the written word as a harnessed thought and how that thought would impact water crystals. He placed labels on bottles of water that expressed human emotions and ideas, some positive and some negative such as "Thank you", "Love", "You make me sick", and "I will kill you". There is no measurable physical action in these experiments, and yet the water crystals responded to the words – positive messages created beautiful geometric crystals, whilst negative messages created malformed or chaotic crystals. Dr. Emoto's experiments have been repeated by many research groups in more controlled circumstances, often with statistically significant results. These experiments show the power of the written word over reality, for each word contains the vibrational frequency of our consciousness.

Numerology

Within Pagan practice the most common understanding of sound vibration is likely to come from the field of numerology. Within numerology we learn that each letter is a set symbol for a sound, that each sound has a set rate of vibration that can be scientifically measured, and that each vibrational measurement uses a number to represent it. Every letter's numbered place in the alphabet *is* its rate of vibration. By using numerology we learn to uncover the vibration and energetic influence of particular words. This can be an excellent tool for the practitioner to harness a particular rate of vibration or to invoke a certain energy during ritual.

Through conscious awareness of the words that we use and the vibrational frequency they contain, we can tailor our words to better reflect our intent and Will. However, the Pagan practitioner may not have, nor need, a full understanding of the many and varied theories regarding sound and vibration, yet can still appreciate the importance of language during ritual. Experimentation with tone, pitch, rhyme, alliteration, inflection, tempo, harmony and song, can all yield some interesting energetic results. Starting with simple chants we can easily feel the difference between a short, sharp chant that increases our heart rate and sends blood rushing around our body, and a gentle, flowing chant that lowers our blood pressure and clears our mind. Both styles may raise energy, but they do so in very different ways and have very different influences on our physical form.

Speeches that have gone down in history do so because of the incredible impact they have on the mental and emotional state of the listeners, and may also have tapped into magical techniques that create resonance with the energy of the crowd. Matching the tempo and rhythm of such speeches, as well as utilizing changes in pitch and tone, may replicate the impact felt by the listeners.

Using melody and harmony can create gentle but definite physical and emotional response for the magical practitioner, one only has to listen to Gregorian chanting or pitch-perfect unaccompanied singing and witness the physical reaction of goosebumps arising on your skin or tears welling in your eyes to understand the power of sound affecting the physical. With the ever-increasing literacy within our world, language both written and verbal may have lost its sense of magic and secrecy, but as practitioners who seek the deeper mysteries we will uncover and understand the essence of language as an expression of intent, Will, and creation.

Techniques for Weaving Words of Power

Repetition

Repetition in ritual is a common technique for raising awareness and energy, either by repeating particular sounds or words, or by repeating entire chants. Repetition is a unifying device used in all poetry, with repetition of sound, syllable, word, phrase, line, stanza, or metrical pattern, and can be found in religious chants of many cultures. In fact, repetition can often reinforce or even replace the meter in poetry, creating a rhythm that develops into cadence or song. Repeating a particular word or phrase implies importance to the conscious mind and builds upon the ideal or concept the repeating phrase or word portrays.

Alliteration

Alliteration is a form of repetition using a singular sound at the beginning of several words within a sentence, and is also known as "front rhyme". This form of repetition can be very catchy, and serves as a great method of remembering a chant or invocation. It is a technique often employed by marketing and advertising companies, because quite honestly it works.

Aside from the practical application of assisting us in remembering our ritual words, alliteration also offers us the opportunity to harness the energetic influence of a particular sound by layering that sound over and over. This technique can be tied into others, such as numerology, by searching for a single letter or sound that encompasses some aspect of your ritual or magical working and then using that to create the words of your ritual. Consciously harness the energy you desire by starting each word or phrase with that energy and repeating it throughout your ritual.

Rhyme

Rhyme is one of the most commonly used techniques in ritual

writing, although in some sense that can be unfortunate. I have seen practitioners attempt to work within rhyming couplets and as a result their desire to "make it fit" actually harms the content of their work. It is, in my honest opinion, a far better thing to write with conscious awareness of what you say and how you say it than to try to use words that offer you a rhyme and no more. Of course, for those who have a natural ability with language, rhyming beautifully and also conveying the exact message they wish to may seem an easy task – but it is not for everyone.

Rhyming is a fantastic tool for oral traditions to pass on information, as the mind more easily remembers and recalls the repetition of rhyme than of plain prose. Rhyming couplets have often been used in theater to bind or end a scene or an act, as a way of signifying the completion, importance or release of the actions previously portrayed. Within magic, rhymes are often used in spellcraft in a similar manner of binding and completing the energy. Again, rhyme is a form of repetition, although more commonly found in the words or syllables at the end of a sentence. This sound then becomes your end note, the final point of reference for the energy you are raising. As such, it is important that the repetition of your final sound be relevant to your magical workings.

Tempo

Tempo is usually considered a musical term, but it also relates to the speed or pace evident in your ritual words. Chanting is a prime example of tempo in action. Many chants will start slowly, with clear and evenly paced words. The pace may increase gradually, or with each round of the chant becoming more rapid, and may also be accompanied by vigorous hand clapping, stamping, dancing or drumming. The tempo increases to the point of impossibility, when it is no longer possible to maintain the speed of the chant with speech, and the frenetic energy raised is released in a crescendo of sound or a sudden silence.

Pay close attention to the tempo of your words, for it will greatly affect the emotional state and energy levels of ritual participants. Be practical too, a long-winded chant will not work well if you intend to increase the tempo to raise energy. Tempo can be measured by beats per minute, the same way your heart rate is measured, and the two are linked. The faster paced chants will increase your heart rate as your body seeks to match the tempo of your chant, and conversely you can create a calming effect upon the body if you consciously design a slow-paced chant.

Reading your words aloud is a good way of discovering the natural tempo of your text, and if you seek to increase or decrease the tempo you can experiment by reading aloud, changing the pace and listening to how your own body reacts.

Rhythm

Rhythm is the pattern of speech and silence, the dance of ebb and flow within your words. In language, rhythm is all about timing. Using techniques of rhyme and alliteration can produce a particular rhythm naturally, but you can also use a conscious method of pausing at intervals to invoke an ebb and flow of energy. A good rhythm can be very hypnotic, and can bring about a sense of trance or otherworldliness to both the speaker and the listener.

Rhythm and tempo both play important roles in guided meditation, allowing the body to relax and the mind to alter its state of awareness comfortably. If a meditation lacks rhythm, the mind constantly jumps back into conscious awareness, but a gentle rhythm acts like a lullaby to a baby and soothes the soul with safety and security.

The Sound of Silence

Vocalization of our intent and Will is very important within ritual, but so is silence. Silence allows the sound vibrations you produce to hang in the air, to be accepted and absorbed by nature, or to be returned in echoed frequency. Silence gives us the chance to connect with and release the energy we are raising, and offers us the opportunity of hearing and feeling the Divine response to our energetic influence.

Silence is also impossible. Even when we stop speaking, our body and spirit hum with the billions of vibrations that make up the cells of our physical and spiritual existence. With or without speech, we are a symphony of sound. Silencing our words allows us time to focus on the energy that we are sharing with the world through our very act of being, and gives us a better understanding of our thoughts and the interaction of our consciousness with the universe around us.

Song: Tone, Pitch, Key

Singing, with or without musical accompaniment, is a fabulous method of combining many different sound techniques in one form. The art of singing as a connection to the Divine can be found in many cultures throughout history, and it is easy to see how the Divine inspires such beautiful, enduring and uplifting melodies. If you have an aptitude for music, I would strongly suggest that you explore the possibility of creating a ritual of sound, music and song. Song allows us to utilize different vibrational frequencies at the same time, by harnessing the sound vibration created by the tone and pitch of the singer, and by harnessing the sound vibration of the word itself. With song, there is endless variation and combination of sound vibration, and an opportunity of layering frequencies through the art of harmonizing with others.

Resonance

Resonance is the physics effect of periodic intervals of a frequency matching and amplifying the frequency of oscillation of a structure. The energy is stored within the structure and increases the rate of vibration. This effect can be seen in the dramatic examples of opera singers producing vocals that exactly replicate the frequency of a glass, causing the glass to vibrate at an ever increasing rate until the structure collapses and shatters. Resonance is taken into account during the building of structures such as bridges, for important reasons. The dramatic and terrifying collapse of the Takoma Bridge is an example of large scale resonance in action, with a simple shift in air current causing a seemly solid and stable structure to ripple and bend.

Resonance in ritual can be used to increase and amplify the energy you are raising, and can be as simple as the use of a single sound such as "Om" repeated in tone and duration to build and increase the energy, or the layering of sounds from singing bowls that resonate in varying frequencies. The art of effectively using resonance can build powerful spirals of energy that deeply affect both the physical and spiritual forms.

The word resonance has also slipped into modern usage to explain the deep connection we feel with a concept or idea. This too is an energetic concept. As Dr. Emoto shows us through his experiments with water, a concept or idea carries its own energetic vibration and as such it is perfectly reasonable that we can resonate with it and feel its truth, when we recognize, accept and amplify the energy.

Language as Creation

In the beginning there was the Word, and the Word was with God, and the Word was God.

Many creation myths begin with the word, a sound, a vibration that sparks the creation of all things. Even the scientific principle starts with a Big Bang, the sound impact of which we are still discovering and learning about in our amazing universe. We too are creators of reality, and it is our words, our sound vibrations, that manifest change. We, as magical practitioners, must be aware of both the definition and meaning of our chosen words and their root energy to shape our spells or rituals, and understand that the act of combining words to create our rituals is an act of magic in itself. Words are sounds, sounds are vibration, vibration is energy, energy is magic. The language of ritual is the art of creation through vibration.

Purification

Ritual bathing, self purification or group-based purification rites done prior to the ritual circle casting are common practice in many paths. The word purification somehow implies that we are spiritually impure, dirty or even sinful, and I believe that is an unfortunate interpretation of the word. In no way does a purification rite imply that we need to be rid of our sins as if we are somehow unfit for the presence of the Divine; it is an act of cleansing away any doubt, fear, stress or anxiety to better focus our minds on the task ahead. Just as our skin becomes dirty through our daily activities, just as our bodies hold the tension and stresses of our interactions, our minds also become cluttered and murky.

Techniques like this aid our connection to the Divine by clearing our cluttered thoughts, relieving stress and leaving us relaxed and ready to welcome the sacredness of experience. It is a psychological process as well as a spiritual one, allowing us to better step from the mundane to the magical. If I have the time and the facilities, I adore a full ritual bath. I usually add salt and sage to cleanse and purify, although I occasionally tailor my bath to the season or reason of my ritual by adding associated pure essential oils and herbs. A long soak not only does the body the world of good, it really allows the mind time to meditate on any issues that arise and let go of any unwarranted stress. If the issues that arise during meditation require further attention, there is an opportunity to face these issues and seek guidance during the ritual ahead.

A common method of group purification rites is the art of using burning incense, sage or sweetgrass to smudge each participant prior to entering the circle. Smudging with sage appears very Native American in style, but you only have to watch the swinging censer moving along the aisle of a Catholic Church to realize that the sacred art of cleansing and purifying with smoke crosses time, continents and spiritual paths. It is well worth investing the time and energy to experiment with creating your own ritual blends of traditional resin-based incense.

Alternatively, anointing with sacred oils prior to entering the circle is another technique. This is usually done by the High Priest and High Priestess of the coven or group, firstly anointing each participant upon the forehead and secondly either challenging the participants' intentions or requesting the "password" as the participant seeks entry to the circle. Again, creating your own ritual blends of purification oils is a worthy practice, improving your understanding of the physical, mental, emotional and spiritual effects of each essential oil.

The following poetry and prose offers a selection of purification blessings and techniques for solitary or group practice.

Purification of Self
Blessed be this water
Cleansing body
Refreshing the soul
Washing the mind clean
Preparing me for the rite ahead

Water Blessing
As I wash my hands of the day's troubles
I wash my body of the day's tiredness
I wash my face of worry
I feel blessed, refreshed, awake and alive
Water to carry away negativity
Water to bring in positivity
Water to bless me

Anointing
HPS: I anoint thee in the name of the Lord and Lady.

Blessed be.

Participant: Blessed be.

HPS: How do you enter this circle?

Participant: In perfect love and perfect trust.

Shower Cleansing

Wash away the stress and strain
Wash away the hurt and pain
Refresh and cleanse my tired soul
To reconnect, to make me whole

Formal Self-Purification

I am a child of this world
With all that it means
I am a child of spirit
With all that it means
I cleanse my body
I cleanse my mind
I cleanse my heart
I cleanse my soul
Each aspect refreshed and blessed
In harmony, in rest
I face the future with love and trust
To do all I can, and all I must

Cleansing Another

I bless you in the name of the Lord and Lady
I cleanse you in the name of the Lord and Lady
Put down your troubles
Lighten your heart
Enter the circle
On a sacred path
So mote it be

Smudge Blessing

Lighter than air
Troubles rise
From earth to the skies
Be free, at peace
A mind at rest
Blessed

Cleansing and Consecrating

Cleansing and consecrating are the first steps to any traditional ritual-based circle casting, coven or solitary. To cleanse a space is to free ourselves and the environment of any residual unwanted energies, and may also include the physical act of tidying and cleaning the area you are about to use. This is important when the area about to be used for ritual purposes also has another daily function. Cleaning and tidying is practical, but so is clearing out any lingering energies associated with the usual use of the room or space. Anyone who has walked into a room where an argument recently occurred and can still feel the tension in the air, will understand how important it is to energetically cleanse an environment to create a space free from those potentially influential residual energies.

In Wicca and many paths of Witchcraft the cleansing usually takes the form of sweeping the circle with a besom, from inside the circle to outside of the circle area, which provides the added benefit of a physical sweep as well as a metaphysical sweeping. When working within a group the visual act of sweeping not only prepares the space, but also serves to prepare the minds of the individuals within the group. Instinctively each person sweeps their minds as the circle is swept, assisting in ridding themselves of the day's stress, anxiety or cluttered thought. Some practitioners will energetically cleanse as they physically sweep, others use a separate technique such as smudging with sage or incense, sprinkling with salt water, scattering a circle of herbs, banging drums, ringing bells, or walking around the circle with a representation of each element.

Consecrating is the act of making a space sacred, and can be as simple as declaring your intent to use this place as a sacred space. Many practitioners will combine a consecration into their actions of cleansing, using language and energetic thought to define the use of the space as a sacred place for ritual.

Some spiritual paths see no need to cast a circle, or to cleanse and consecrate a space prior to a ritual or celebration. To many, including myself, the whole world is sacred. As such, why define a sacred space at all? The process of cleansing space and casting circle does not denote that one space is sacred and another is not, but it does create an energetic space between the worlds for the practitioner to work within.

Wicca and many forms of Witchcraft teach that a circle not only provides a protective boundary for the practitioners within, but it also holds and contains any power raised until the point of release. I personally believe a circle provides many more functions, not least that by defining a sacred space in which to work we are psychologically preparing ourselves to step back from our mundane lives and accept the sacredness of all life – including our own. The boundary that we create not only protects the practitioners within, but also protects people and spirits outside from the magic raised within the circle. The magic of ritual is a bright welcoming light on a dark night, and like moths to a flame many spirits and energies are attracted to its light. A ritual circle acts like a glass around a flame – it stops those attracted to the light from being harmed.

The technique and method of casting a circle also mentally creates a sense of seriousness, a sense of importance, something that is removed from our everyday existence. Ritual, however joyful or celebratory, is still an important time and deserves to be treated seriously, with respect and with reverence. During ritual a practitioner stands naked, sometimes literally but always figuratively. They are exposed, vulnerable, in their purest and most honest form, without the masks they wear during the different roles of their lives. This deserves respect and under-standing. A circle not only offers the practitioner a sacred space, it also offers a safe place, a place where we can be who we are in our entirety without societal masks.

Dependant on the practitioner, their path and the particular working they are doing at the time, they may choose to cast a full ritual circle, calling quarters and evoking or invoking deity, or simply create an energetic boundary to work within. They may choose to cleanse prior to creating their boundary, or they may not have the time or desire to do so.

For those who feel a cleansing is appropriate for ritual, or for those who wish to incorporate the practice of cleansing into other aspects of their craft, the following chants, poems and prose offer a selection of cleansings and consecrations either individually or combined.

Basic Sweep

Sweep away stress and strife,
Sweep away negativity,
Replace the void with peace and love,
Replace the void with positivity.

Sweep and Consecrate

Sweep and clear
Be gone from here
Shift darkness from heart and mind
Bless this space
A sacred place
A time outside of time

Basic Sweep II

As I sweep the circle in to out
May the besom clear our path ahead
Sweep away the negativity
Leave room for joy instead

Physical and Mental Sweep

As I sweep, may this place be cleansed

From all debris of mind and heart
Chase away the negativity
Sweep and clear my path

Sweep and Consecrate II

Sweep and cleanse!
Sweep and clear!
Chase away all doubt and fear
Sweep the circle!
Sweep this place!
Soon to be a sacred space

Preparation Sweep

As I wield a broom of old
I do more than sweep the floor
I chase away the negativity
And push it out the door
Begone!
Begone!
There is work to be done

Order from Chaos

As I sweep, may this besom clear away all unwanted energies,
Bring order from chaos,
And cleanse the space ready for my ritual work

Cleanse of Space

There is work to be done
Divine will to shape
Sweep away the negativity
Cleanse this sacred space

Sweep and Cleanse

My hand upon the besom guides away all unwanted,

unneeded energies
My hand upon the besom clears and cleanses this space
By my hand, by my will
I sweep and cleanse ready for the blessings of the Divine

By my Hand

By my hand, by my will
I clear this place of all its ills
By my will, by my hand
I make a sacred space of this land

Samhain Cleansing

The wheel turns, as we turn
We spiral into darkness, deep and complete
Stripping away all to truth and bone
Clearing the way in one fell sweep

Circle Casting

My circle is a sphere, above me, below me, around me. It is a boundary without bounds, forming within, through and around walls, floors and ceilings, furniture and fabric, earth and air, water, tree and stone. It is pure energy harnessed and shaped into a moving, flowing, shifting barrier of protection. It is the air I breathe, the sunlight that warms me, the dew on the grass and the ground that I walk upon. It is the shape of my Will. It is the shape of my need. It is the shape of creation. It is the turning of our planet, and the spiral dance of planets and stars, stars and galaxies, galaxies and universe. It is the essence of all from the smallest particle to the largest planet, from the cells of my body to the spheres of my thought. It is without beginning or end, infinite in its energetic flow. It is all around us, all the time, fluid and flowing. With heart and hand, Will and wisdom, power and blade, I channel the energy through me and around me, directing its dance of chaos and creation into a choreographed dance of form and purpose. The energy spirals out and around me, following my thought, my Will, and creating an energetic line in the sands of every plane of existence. Within this sacred space that straddles time and worlds, I raise more energy for ritual intent, for celebration, for healing, for change. The energy I raise is contained within my boundary, the circle I have created gently and firmly ushering the spiral of frenetic energy seeking to rush away to fulfill its purpose, with whispers of patience, patience, your time will come, soon you will be released. The energy and entities of the world outside my boundary are just as gently and firmly told to move along, nothing to see here, go about your business. Safe inside, I trust my circle to complete its task of protection, to protect all within and all without, to dance the fine line of allowing the necessary energies of nature to affect my space whilst repelling undesired energetic influences. I cast, I

create and I trust. My circle is a sphere, above me, below me and
all around me.

Circle Between Worlds
In this space without a place,
In a time outside of time,
Between the worlds of Gods and Man
We form our sacred circle of Divine intent
So mote it be

Simple Protection
I cast this circle in love and light
And ask for protection in this rite
By East and West, North and South
From magic within cast circle without

Circle of Power
By Divine Will
I Conjure Thee
A Circle of Power
To protect me
By East and West
North and South
From Power Within
I Cast Circle Without
As Above, 'tis So Below

Simple Healing Circle
By my Will
I conjure in
A circle of healing
For all within
As I will it, so mote it be

Element Healing Circle

By Earth's regeneration
By sweeping, rushing Air
By the cleansing Fire
By purity of Water
I manifest a sacred place
Of hope and healing
Take form
By my Will
So mote it be

Strong as Stone

I cast about this place
A circle as strong as stone
A circle to keep out ills
A circle to keep out harm
A circle to protect all within
I raise you like a wall, surround us all
Follow thought and now begin
So mote it be

Formal Circle I

I draw a circle of power in this consecrated space
Above me, below me, around me
Through objects and earth and air
This circle is formed in strength and wisdom
With the elements of all, and the presence of the Divine
By my Will, this circle is cast
So mote it be

By Power of the Elements

I cast about this sacred space a circle of power
By the energy and elements of all that be
By sand, and sky, and sun, and sea

By Divine spirit external and within me
Above me, below me, around me
The boundary of my circle is cast
So mote it be

Formal Circle II

Here lies the boundary of my circle
Formed through matter and spirit
Only those with knowledge of the password are welcome here
In love and trust
In will and wisdom
By the power of the Divine that lies in me
I cast in strength and form in love
As I will it, so mote it be

Formal Circle III

I conjure thee
Circle of power
That you may be a boundary between the worlds
That you may be a place between times
That you may protect those within its walls
That you may contain the power raised within
I bless and consecrate thee in the essence of the elements
I bless and consecrate thee in the names of the Lord and Lady
Be formed now in strength and love
So mote it be

Sphere of Protection

I draw this circle about me, in the presence of the elements
   and Divine spirit
That I may be aided by the Lord and Lady and be blessed by
   my work this night
The boundary of my circle lies below my feet,
Above my head

Around my body
That I may work within a sphere of protection and love
And protection and love may work within me
The circle is charged and cast, so mote it be

Consecrated by Spirit

I cast a circle of power above and below, inside and outside,
    around and about me
Strengthened by Earth,
Formed by Air,
Charged by Fire,
Cleansed by Water,
Consecrated by Spirit,
As above, 'tis so below
This circle is cast

Universal Circle

As the planets turn and circle one another
In the universal dance of infinity
I turn and circle this place of power
And create a boundary of universal energy
Within and around
Magic abounds
In the dance of eternal creation
Universal I am
Cyclical I am
A tool of transformation
I hold this space
A sacred place
A cauldron of manifestation
Now at last
The circle cast
By my will and invocation

Feminine Mysteries Circle

By the earthly body of my flesh,
The air of my breath,
The fire of my spirit,
The living waters of my womb,
I cast this circle in honor of the Goddess that birthed us all,
And the Goddess within me
Be now a place of power and peace
Consecrated and sacred to all within
As I will it, so shall it be

Simple Casting

As above, 'tis so below
As the Universe, so the soul
As without, 'tis so within
Circle cast, rite begins

Veil Thin

I cast about this place
A circle veil thin
To straddle time and space
To honor all within
In every shifting plane
In all times and none
I cast a sacred space
From earth below to sky above
So mote it be

Quarter Call and Circle Casting I

In fertile fields and woodland shrines
In wild storms and winds benign
Desire and passion in a burning flame
Oceans deep from one drop of rain
We sing:

Earth, Air, Fire, Water
Protections formed and never falter
Blessed be

Quarter Call and Circle Casting II

Mountains high to valleys deep,
Bitter winds to gentle breeze,
Heat of heart to heat of flame,
Oceans wide to drop of rain,
Earth Air Fire Water,
From power within, my world to alter
So mote it be.

Quarter Call and Circle Casting III

The rushing winds form this circle. The spring of our youth forms this circle. The whispered wisdom forms this circle. The breath of our bodies forms this circle.

The flames of transformation form this circle. The summer of life forms this circle. The passion of living forms this circle. The heat of our bodies form this circle.

The rivers of belief form this circle. The autumn of our maturity forms this circle. The ebb and flow of energy forms this circle. The joy and sadness of our tears form this circle.

The cycle of life, death and rebirth forms this circle. The winter of our life forms this circle. The knowledge of magic forms this circle. The power and presence we bear forms this circle.

Calling the Quarters / Four Directions: Elements, Elementals, Guardians

Calling the quarters varies dramatically depending on which path the practitioner walks, from very earthy folk magic (low magic) of harnessing the energy of the elements around you, to the ceremonial (high magic) practice of summoning the Guardians of the watchtowers, the Angels or even opening portals to Elemental realms. Some paths make no particular reference to calling the quarters, although many will still work with or harness the energy of the four directions and the elements during the course of their rituals.

Personally, I keep it simple. When creating the circle I will most often call to the elements of our world, harnessing not only the energy of earth, air, fire and water, but also invoking the qualities of each element to better strengthen my connection to spirit. If I require interactive assistance, I will call to the Elementals, the sentient energetic beings composed of and dwelling within each element. Rarely, unless working with a group or seeking particular assistance, do I summon or call any other kind of Guardian.

If you are still discovering your path, there is nothing wrong with just working with the elements. The elements are the foundation of our world and of our magic, so learning to work with them effectively is one of the most important lessons you can master. If you are training within a coven, grove or group and they do things differently, you may learn to work with Angels or Guardians from the outset. All paths are valid in their own way. There are many paths up the mountain, but the destination remains the same.

Learn all you can about the different ways of calling the quarters; understand as best you can what they bring to your circle and your craft. Ask questions, read books, attend rituals and experience. You will soon learn what feels right to you, and you will also learn to get support and work differently if you feel out of your depth. Above all else, be respectful. Understand that you are but one part of the sacred experience and when working with other energies or entities they too play an important role. Together you can work wondrous magic, but learning how to work together is magic in and of itself.

Below I offer a simple selection of poetry and prose to call the quarters and work with the four directions. With a little research or inspiration these can also be adapted to suit your individual path.

Familial Elements

Mother Earth, Sister Water, Brother Fire, Father Air
I bid you to come, I beg you to hear
In perfect trust I call to thee
I seek your help, So Blessed Be.

Element Effects

With earth we learn a new way
With the wind we sing a new day
With the fire we burn to survive
With water we respect our lives
Hail and welcome to the elements of our world

Moon River Quarter Calls

Powers of North and Earth
Of fertile field and woodland shrine
Gift us with strength and fertility
For the duration of this rite
Hail and welcome

Powers of East and Air
Of wild storms and winds benign

Gift us with intellect and creativity
For the duration of this rite
Hail and welcome

Powers of South and Fire
Of burning flame that lights the night
Gift us with passion and virility
For the duration of this rite
Hail and welcome

Powers of West and Water
Of oceans deep and tears of mine
Gift us with love and empathy
For the duration of this rite
Hail and welcome

Element Qualities I

I call upon North and Earth to lend stability to this rite
I call upon East and Air to lend inspiration to this rite
I call upon South and Fire to lend desire to this rite
I call upon West and Water to lend purity to this rite

Element Qualities II

I call upon the power of Earth to bring strength to this rite
I call upon the power of Air to bring clarity to this rite
I call upon the power of Fire to bring focus to this rite
I call upon the power of Water to bring wisdom to this rite

Element Guardians

Hail to the Guardians of Earth
We welcome you to our sacred space
May your earthly wisdom and experience bring forth such
    qualities in us
As we honor the Divine this night

Hail and welcome!

Hail to the Guardians of Air
We welcome you to our sacred space
May your inspiration and intellect bring forth such qualities
    in us
As we honor the Divine this night
Hail and welcome

Hail to the Guardians of Fire
We welcome you to our sacred space
May your burning passion and desire bring forth such
    qualities in us
As we honor the Divine this night
Hail and welcome

Hail to the Guardians of Water
We welcome you to our sacred space
May your empathy and understanding bring forth such
    qualities in us
As we honor the Divine this night
Hail and welcome

Direction and Element I

Greetings and blessings to North and Earth,
By dark of night I welcome thee
In cycles of seasons forever changing
I accept your influence within and around me
I seek you out and call your name
To be with me on this sacred night
May your qualities be found within me
And your blessings be bestowed upon this rite

Greetings and blessings to East and Air,

By break of dawn I welcome thee
In breeze and storms and winds of change
I accept your influence within and around me
I seek you out and call your name
To be with me on this sacred night
May your qualities be found within me
And your blessings be bestowed upon this rite

Greetings and blessings to South and Fire,
By heat of day I welcome thee
In forging fires of transformation
I accept your influence within and around me
I seek you out and call your name
To be with me on this sacred night
May your qualities be found within me
And your blessings be bestowed upon this rite

Greetings and blessings to West and Water,
By peace of dusk I welcome thee
In ebb and flow and tides of change
I accept your influence within and around me
I seek you out and call your name
To be with me on this sacred night
May your qualities be found within me
And your blessings be bestowed upon this rite

Direction and Element II
Greetings and blessings to North and Earth
Mother of all and womb of manifestation
I welcome your strength and stability
In my circle this night
May you be at home in the sanctuary of my arms

Greetings and blessings to East and Air

Father of word and whispered wisdom
I welcome your thought and inspiration
In my circle this night
May you be at ease in the sanctuary of my mind

Greetings and blessings to South and Fire
Brother of destruction, creation and transformation
I welcome your passion and vitality
In my circle this night
May you be in comfort in the sanctuary of my spirit

Greetings and blessings to West and Water
Sister of life and emotional tides
I welcome your purity and understanding
In my circle this night
May you be at peace in the sanctuary of my heart

Winter's Elements

Hail to the element of North and Earth
Of mountains and valleys
Of forest and stone
Of bitter winter
Of hearth and home
We welcome your presence in our rite
As we gather upon this sacred night
Hail and welcome

Hail to the element of East and Air
Of thought and voice
Of breeze and gale
Of flight and freedom
Of winter's wail
We welcome your presence in our rite
As we gather upon this sacred night

Hail and welcome

Hail to the element of South and Fire
Of desire and love
Of rage and ire
Of burning sun
Of winter fires
We welcome your presence in our rite
As we gather upon this sacred night
Hail and welcome

Hail to the element of West and Water
Of raging river
Of quiet streams
Of frozen lakes
Of bitter sea
We welcome your presence in our rite
As we gather upon this sacred night
Hail and welcome

Calling the Elementals I

I call upon the Elementals of Earth
Hear me now Gnomes of peaks and valleys, mountain and
    cave
I request your presence during this rite
By my strength and physical form, we are kith and kin
Be with me now my family, at my time of need

I call upon the Elementals of Air
Hear me now Sylphs of gentle breeze and wild storms
I request your presence during this rite
By my thought and breath of word, we are kith and kin
Be with me now my family, at my time of need

I call upon the Elementals of Fire
Hear me now Salamanders of burning flame
I request your presence during this rite
By my passion and will to live, we are kith and kin
Be with me now my family, at my time of need

I call upon the Elementals of Water
Hear me now Undines of river and sea
I request your presence during this rite
By my blood and emotional tides, we are kith and kin
Be with me now my family, at my time of need

Guardians of the Directions

Hail to the Guardians of the North
Protectors of earth and physical manifestations
I call upon your presence and power
To bear witness to my rite
Bless me with your presence in this sacred space
During this time outside of time
Hail to thee, and welcome be

Hail to the Guardians of the East
Protectors of air and manifestations of thought
I call upon your presence and power
To bear witness to my rite
Bless me with your presence in this sacred space
During this time outside of time
Hail to thee, and welcome be

Hail to the Guardians of the South
Protectors of fire and manifestations of Will
I call upon your presence and power
To bear witness to my rite
Bless me with your presence in this sacred space

During this time outside of time
Hail to thee, and welcome be

Hail to the Guardians of the West
Protectors of water and emotional manifestations
I call upon your presence and power
To bear witness to my rite
Bless me with your presence in this sacred space
During this time outside of time
Hail to thee, and welcome be

Calling the Elementals II

Hail to the Gnomes of Earth
Of flesh and bone, mud and mountain
Bring the gift of a solid foundation
To the magic woven within this rite
Welcome to my circle

Hail to the Sylphs of Air
Of breath and thought, breeze and gale
Bring the gift of inspiration and knowledge
To the magic woven within this rite
Welcome to my circle

Hail to the Salamanders of Fire
Of heart and blood, light and flame
Bring the gift of a focused Will
To the magic woven within this rite
Welcome to my circle

Hail to the Undines of Water
Of hormonal tides, sea and stream
Bring the gift of simple truth
To the magic woven within this rite

Welcome to my circle

Calling the Autumn / Harvest Elements

I call upon the blessings and energy of North and Earth! Blessings manifest in the fruits of the harvest, in the crops and corn, in the giving earth, and in the soil we stand upon. Share with us the mystery of bounty, of growth and diversity. Gift us with your qualities. Be with us now during this blessed rite; be with us now as we celebrate the Divine. Hail and welcome!

I call upon the blessings and energy of East and Air! Blessings manifest within the sharing of knowledge, in the scattering of seed, in the whispering corn fields, and in the gentle breeze. Share with us the mystery of inspiration, of connection and communication. Gift us with your qualities. Be with us now during this blessed rite; be with us now as we celebrate the Divine. Hail and welcome!

I call upon the blessings and energy of South and Fire! Blessings manifest in the sun-ripened earth, in the warmth of skin, in the abundant sun, and in the fire within. Share with us the mystery of wax and wane, of shadow and flame. Gift us with your qualities. Be with us now during this blessed rite; be with us now as we celebrate the Divine. Hail and welcome!

I call upon the blessings and energy of West and Water! Blessings manifest in the taste of sweet fruits, in the thirst slaked, in the rain-washed fields, and in the bountiful lakes. Share with us the mystery of rise and subside, of emotional tides. Gift us with your qualities. Be with us now during this blessed rite; be with us now as we celebrate the Divine. Hail and welcome!

Requiem Rite Quarter Calls

Our tears like the salt waters of the ocean's ebb and flow, our hearts spill with emotion. We seek the blessing of water's presence, to lend clarity, honesty, and healing to this rite. Find home in our hearts, comfort in our tears, and love within our grief. Be with us in our hour of need. Blessed be.

As the sun sets upon the day and darkness falls, so does a light leave our lives with the passing of Our Beloved. We seek the blessings of fire to kindle old memories to burn bright, to scatter the embers of love into each heart and warm us in the cold dark nights of grief. Find a home in our hearts, comfort in our community, and love within our grief. Be with us in our hour of need. Blessed be.

As the breath of life leaves Our Beloved and whispers out into the universe, so do we whisper our words of love and loss, gratitude and grief out into the universe. We seek the blessings of Air to communicate our thoughts and feelings, our hopes and dreams, beyond this space and into the realms of spirit. Find a home in our hearts, comfort in our words, and love within our grief. Be with us in our hour of need. Blessed be.

As the earth blesses us with the cycles of life and death, so do we celebrate the life and mourn the death of Our Beloved. We seek the blessings of earth to bring understanding of life and death, to welcome Our Beloved back to the earth, and to lend us the strength to endure our grief. Find a home in our hearts, comfort in our remembrance, and love within our grief. Be with us in our hour of need. Blessed be.

Charge of Earth

Be still, for I am Earth

My body is the womb of the world
My pulse the beat beneath your feet
I move the mountains
I am the mountains
I am the valley
I am the stone
I am the old one that births all life
I am all life
I am first of all
I am all within all
My body encircles all
Be still and listen, for I am Earth

Charge of Air

Listen, for I am Air
My voice is swift and boundless
Whispered in the subtle dawn greeting
Screamed upon the sudden storm
I am cold and keen
I am the kiss of gentle breeze
I am one within all
For I am the breath of life
I am the first word
I am the last word
I am the first breath
I am the last breath
Listen and breathe, for I am Air

Charge of Fire

Behold, I am fire
I am light and life
I am the spark that ignites
I am the burning that consumes
I transform all that I touch

I am warmth and hope in darkness
I am the flame
I am the inferno
I am the blazing sun
I am hurt and healing
I am illumination
Behold me and listen, for I am Fire

Charge of Water

Hear me, for I am Water
My voice is the patter of rainfall, the hiss of ocean spray
My still waters the reflection of your soul
I reach you in the rush of river and turning tide
I am the surging waves and the gentle surf upon shore
I am the boundless, bountiful sea
I am the hidden depths
I am the waters of the womb
I am the cradle of life rocked by Lady Luna's hand
I am the blood of life feeding all the Earth
I am in all life
I am all
Feel me and listen, for I am Water

Divine Invocations and Evocations

To many women the Goddess speaks, and the God whispers. To many men, the God speaks and the Goddess whispers. It is the skill of the practitioner to listen.

There are several schools of thought around the terms "invocation" and "evocation", which I believe will require clarification to better understand the following sections of poetry and prose. To many groups the term invocation implies a request of presence to Divine aspects, and evocation a command of energies and spiritual entities. This is not what I was taught. During my studies I was always taught that any request of presence, regardless of energetic form, should be done with respect and awareness of interconnection. To call to energy, to work with energy, to align energy, to direct energy, and to choreograph energy, but to do so with reverence and respect, not demands and expectations.

In my school of training the difference between invocation and evocation lies not in the method of *request,* but in the method of *presence.* To evoke is to request the presence within your ritual space, to invite into one's vicinity. To invoke is to request the presence within oneself, to bring elements, Elementals, energies or the Divine into yourself, to be host through your physical body. An easy way to remember is this: Evoke is External, INvoke is INternal. It is most common to evoke during ritual, and for anyone new to ritual practice I would certainly suggest this as a first course of action.

The art of invoking and evoking lies not just in the words you use to invite presence, but in the way you utilize your voice. The world is a noisy place, full of the sounds of hopes, dreams, wishes and prayers of billions. The world is a crowded ballroom of glitz and glitter, laughter, debate and conversations, and you are but one person seeking attention within the din. The art lies not in raising one's voice and shouting for attention, but in creating uniqueness, a difference, and an energetic thread of attraction that quietly but confidently works to turn the heads of those you seek. Like the strains of beautiful music within the babble, the sound of your evocation draws attention towards you. Within the ebb and flow of noise, the jostling bodies, and the many distractions, the Divine hears you call their name and their gaze seeks the reflection of your eyes. You find your divine dancing partner, not with shouted demands, but with sublime invitation.

Any of the following pieces can be quickly adapted to reflect either invocation or evocation depending on your need. Be aware of the language you use to phrase your request, and the impact that will have upon yourself and any other practitioners you are working with.

Invoking and Evoking Deity: Feminine Divine

Gender is in everything; everything has its Masculine and Feminine Principles; Gender manifests on all planes.
— The Kybalion

The Great Goddess, the Feminine Divine, is the female principle and aspect of the Divine All that resides both within us all and external to us all. She wears many faces and has many names, each one unique yet connected to every other aspect. As Goddess she is the creator and destroyer, the nurturer and the warrior. She is the young Maiden, the flowering Mistress, the devoted Priestess and the old Crone. She is the womb of birth and creation, the cauldron of transformation, and the tomb of death and rebirth. She is light, love and laughter; darkness, fear and sorrow. She is with each girl as she journeys to womanhood, and with each woman as she journeys towards death. She is the mystery that resides in the cycles of moon blood, in sex, in pregnancy, in birth, in loss, in grief, in love, in passion, in battle, in teaching and receiving, in learning and growing, in illness and death. She is the muse of artists and poets, the inspiration for progress, and the catalyst for change. She changes everything she touches, and everything she touches changes.

There are times when a practitioner does not feel confident using an unfamiliar or detailed invocation to hail a deity, or when a large group wishes to all be involved with the process of evocation. If for any reason you do not feel that a particular type of invocation will work well for your ritual, remember to explore the many and varied ways of using language within ritual. Instead of spoken word, one can use a repetitive chant, a song, drumming, dancing, or even just the deity name sung over and over as a musical call. I have participated in rituals where every member of the circle sang the deity's name in a simple repetitive melody, their voices layering and overlapping, cresting and falling, and creating the most wonderful energetic call. This can be a truly magical experience, and one in which it is easy to involve many participants – novice or adept.

The selection of invocations and evocations to individual Goddesses that I offer here are all my own creations. These are words woven together from meditation, inspiration and experience, and I feel they are effective and appropriate for each individual deity. However, that does not mean that they will ring true for every practitioner, so please feel free to use them as inspiration to create your own invocations or use them in their entirety if they resonate with you. Please be aware that some are written as invocations and others as evocations, so you will need to review the language used to make sure it is in alignment with your intent and change the language if necessary.

Charge of the Goddess

I am the time outside of time,
And the cycle that time revolves around
I am the spark of life found in all things
Both within this reality and without
I am the laughter of children found in bleak winter cold
I am the tears of lovers drying in the summer sun
I am the desire of youth burning within the old
I am the honest relief found when death comes
I reside in your hopes and fears
And spiral through the lands of your dreams
I am the unforgiving sense of familiarity
When life is no longer as it seems
I am the challenge of every new born life
I am the hunger that still seeks when all are fed
I am the joy discovered after hardness and strife
I am the cold light of truth when lies have been shed

I cannot be called nor coaxed,
Summoned nor stirred,
Begged nor bound,
For I am a part of all things at all times in many ways
I can flow through or form within,
Pass by or pause,
Gather in and gift out,
And speak through you, to you, in honor of the Old Ways

Invoke Goddess (based on a chant by Z Budapest)
We all come from the Goddess
And to her we shall return
Like a drop of rain
Ever flowing to the ocean
We ask that you now join with us
Impart your wisdom and your grace
Passion and fertility now speak
Through the Priestess in your place

Invoke Feminine Divine
Beloved Lady, our Feminine Divine
We ask you here at this time outside of time
To a place of trust and love between
All that is and is yet unseen
Pause a while with us during this rite
Bless us with your wisdom and watchful sight
Let your compassion, experience and grace
Work through this Priestess in your place
Hail and welcome!

Calling the Crone at Samhain
Dark Mother, Grandmother of time and tide,
We welcome you into our hearts and homes.
You have blessed us with your bounty, and now we reap the

spiritual harvest that resides in the dark places of mind and soul.

With your wisdom to guide us, we seek to reveal the secrets of our deepest selves.

With your wisdom to guide us, we seek to honor our ancestors, our beloved dead, and our beloved living.

With your wisdom to guide us, we seek to find comfort and celebration even in the darkest of days and nights.

Old Crone, midwife to the mother of the sun, be with us now as we usher in the new year.

Charge of the Crone

I am the beauty of dark moon, of dark night, of dusk and twilight, of the long evening of your life.

I am the dark earth beneath your feet, from which all is born and all returns eventually.

I am the flesh and bone, worn well and aged to perfection.

I am courage, freedom, truth and wisdom found in every life lived in honor.

I am transition, rebirth and midwife to the dying.

I was with you at the beginning, and I was the wisdom of elders during your youth.

I will be with you at the end and beyond.

I am Crone, reclaiming the power of age.

I am Crone.

Call of the Crone

I am the dark one as old as time
I challenge all before me
I answer to many names
I wear many faces
I walk with winter's sorrow
I speak with wisdom's breath
In one hand I hold life

In the other I hold death
All will know me at the end of time
Old Crone I was
Old Crone I am
Old Crone I will be

Aphrodite

Greek Goddess Aphrodite, born full grown from the foam of the oceans, is the Goddess of sexual love. She is unapologetic and pure in her sexuality, fully owning the power of feminine desire. For women seeking to understand and develop their sexuality, Aphrodite is a great Goddess to connect with. She assists in developing confidence, strength of self, desire and libido. She is the Patron Goddess of prostitutes, of young love, lust and of pure undiluted desire.

Aphrodite Invocation

Beautiful Aphrodite
I bear all to be with thee
Honest before Divinity
I seek passion deep within me
Fill me
With your sacred sexuality
For I am love and desire, pure and free
Share your wisdom and your grace
With this honored Priestess in your place

Aradia

Daughter of Diana and her twin brother Apollo (in some mythologies the daughter of Diana and Lucifer), Aradia is known as the Witch Goddess most often called to by modern Wiccans and Gardnerian Witches. Aradia came to earth to teach the Witches of her mother's magic, and will reveal mysteries to those who earn her trust. It is said that Aradia first appeared in

Tuscany on August 13th, 1313, and as such she is firmly associated with Italian Witchcraft.

Aradia Evocation

Daughter of the silver moon
Daughter of the blazing sun
Daughter of the ocean's tears
Daughter of the whispering winds
Daughter of shadow
Daughter of light
Daughter of sunrise
Daughter of night
Aradia, Aradia
Born of magic and mystery
I turn my hands to skills of old
To learn the arts and honor thee
Welcome me into your mysteries
Queen of Witches
I call to thee

Arianrhod

Very little mythology remains of Welsh Goddess Arianrhod outside of the Mabinogion, which does not paint the most pleasant image of this deity. In the surviving stories, she appears to be a rather bad tempered mother who disowns her sons, and riddles the life of her son Lleu with challenges. However, her image and name invokes the feeling of a much older, multi-faceted deity, whose energy seems to ever spiral around birth, initiation and reincarnation. In more modern times, Arianrhod has resurfaced in a more benevolent light and is associated as the Goddess of Moon and Stars.

Arianrhod Invocation

Fountains spring forth at my footsteps

A crown of stars spiral around me
I am the silver wheel of the sea
Poets and seers fall before me
All turn their gaze at my light step
Dreams held whispered upon my breath
Virgin I am
Mother I am
Crone I am
Forever turning tide
Of Moon and Sea
Earth and Sky
Silver Wheel I am
Arianrhod I am
Goddess I am

Artemis

The Greek Goddess Artemis is known as the maiden huntress, a lithe athletic young woman whose connection to all things wild makes her a true aspect of nature. She is represented by the crescent moon and, like the Goddess Diana, the crescent moon also represents the hunting bow Artemis carries with her. Artemis is the protector of children and animals, making her a great Goddess to invoke when working with social services, sanctuaries and rescue centers.

Artemis Invocation

Blessed Maiden of the Moon
Hunter of men and beast
Bringer of honest justice
And daughter of peace
Laughter in wilderness
And song of the storm
Queen of the mountains
And the valleys they form

Thou art the protector of life
In forest and plain,
Both Maiden and Mother
Huntress and Prey
In paradox you form within
Both separate and whole
I invoke thee now
Into my body and soul

Astarte

Lunar Goddess Astarte, also known as Ishtar, Ashtart, Athtart, or Ashtoreth, is an ancient Goddess celebrated all over the Middle East from the Bronze Age to modern day. She is most commonly referred to as Astarte, Queen of Heaven, and is the second Goddess acknowledged in the modern Pagan chant "Isis, Astarte, Diana, Hecate, Demeter, Kali, Inanna". She is a Goddess of fertility, sexual love and war, although her aggressively sexual, dominant and war-like attributes have been muted over the centuries and she appears today more as a Goddess of love and fertility. Astarte is associated with the evening star, Venus, and one of her symbols is a star within a circle. Her other symbols are the dove, the lion, the horse and the sphinx.

Astarte Invocation

Blessed Goddess of the silver sea
Blessed Goddess of the shining stars
Blessed Goddess of the changing moon
Blessed Astarte, our Evening Star
I often look towards the skies
At dusk, at dawn, at evening haze
I seek your shining sight and
I am honored by your gaze
Gracious Goddess, strong and wise
Hear a humble Priestess' cries

Hear my pleas, be with me,
Gift me with your qualities
I await your blessings
Queen of Heavens

Athena

Great Goddess Athena is the daughter of Olympian Goddess Metis and God Zeus. Her mother is the Divine aspect of law, knowledge, wisdom and foresight, who passed on these traits to Athena. Her father Zeus gave birth to her martial aspects, but unlike the passionate and raging war God Ares, Athena's skills in battle are disciplined, controlled and won through wisdom and tactic. Athena is a protector and guardian of humanity and civilization, and acts as a wise counsel to all who seek wisdom in difficult situations. She prizes education as the greatest weapon we can possess and will support those seeking to further their knowledge and gain wisdom. Her symbols are the owl and the shield.

Athena Invocation

Mother of the wise
Viewing humankind through owl eyes
Silent as flight
Swift in fight
A warrior within a caring guise
Protector of us all
Holding us within homely walls
Skilled in battle
A beauty with mettle
Holding a gaze to all men enthrall
Inspirer of the finest arts
Gifting the seeking with uplifted hearts
Patroness of the mind
For knowledge to find

Fill me now with your wisdom to impart

Bast

Beautiful, sleek Goddess of cats, Bast is a great Goddess to invoke for fun, frivolity, sexuality and sensuality. She is the Goddess of sacred dance, music, pleasure and feminine mystique. From Egyptian origin her father is the Sun God Ra, although Bast is associated with both Moon and Sun. In her Sun aspect she is associated with the dawn and is called by her names The Light Bearer and Lady of the East. In her Moon aspect she is associated with the cat, and is known as Mother Protector or Lady of the Cats. Her protective attitude is both fierce and maternal, and she has a history of protecting children, relationships and the stability of the home. As a cat she is also known to protect the family abundance of food and drink, so that no one goes hungry. Her symbols are the cat and the sistrum, a metal rattle used in ritual. All invocations and evocations of Bast should be done joyfully, but with reverence.

Bast Invocation

Mistress of both Moon and Sun
Born as dark as starry night
Walked the rivers since time begun
Bringing forth the fires bright
Seeking out the feline
In all the feminine hearts
Reflected within your eyes
The secrets of mystical arts
Bringer of pleasure in touch of skin
Sensuality in sacred dance
Bringer of joy to soul within
Invoker of free choice and wild chance
Gift me with pleasure and plenty
In my life and heart to reside

Gift me strength inside beauty
Bring forth the feline deep inside
I invoke thee Bast
Goddess of Cats

Brigid

One of the most ancient and revered of the Celtic Goddesses, Brigid is a triple aspect deity of the arts and crafts, healing and motherhood. She is often portrayed as three sisters, one of whom is a patron deity of smithcraft, forging and metalwork, another of poetry, art and inspiration; and the third as a great healer, wisewoman and keeper of medicinal knowledge. In her triple aspect she is known as the Three Blessed Ladies of Britain, although she is more commonly referred to as Brigit, Brigid, or Bride (pronounced *breed*).

The name Brigid means "shining one" or "bright arrow", and this reflects Brigid's associations with fire, the coming of the Sun, the coming of spring, determined nature, and the pursuit of knowledge and wisdom. In Kildare, Ireland, a temple was erected to Brigid in which a group of nineteen nuns (or Priestesses) kept a fire eternally lit in her name. Brigid's festival is Imbolc, otherwise known as Oimlich or Candlemas, on the 1st and 2nd of February. This is a festival of returning light to the land and of the coming spring.

At the time of Christianity taking hold in the British Isles it was discovered that Brigid invoked such a strong response in the community she was hard to eradicate and replace with a holy male trinity. As a result Brigid was canonized and became known as Saint Bridget, the midwife to the Virgin Mary, in an attempt to bring the Celtic beliefs in line with the new Christian structure. However, many in the community refused to see Brigid spiritually demoted and associated her directly with Mother Mary, reinforcing Brigid's maternal qualities.

Brigid is a fantastic deity to call upon in complex situations that require "thinking outside the box" due her many skills and experience. She is particularly adept at assisting us in creative endeavors, especially if one is suffering from a block or lack of inspiration. As my patron Goddess I can tell you that she is blunt, honest and forthright, with a quirky sense of humor and a strong belief that we must all learn for ourselves. Her advice is sisterly and nurturing, although sometimes given in riddles, and she will never answer your questions directly – simply inspire you to see things in a new perspective.

Brigid Invocation

One within Three,
Yet all Three within One,
Three Sisters of Fire,
And Mother of the Sun,
Thou art the keeper of secrets,
Forger and weaver,
Eloquent poet,
And ancient healer,
Goddess of Old,
And Saint among men
Smothered to embers,
Yet reborn again
Thou art the fire
But I hold your flame
I am You, You are me
One and the same

Cerridwen

Oh wise woman Cerridwen, within your cauldron you stir the mysteries of magic! The Goddess Cerridwen is often visually portrayed with her symbol of the cauldron. The cauldron represents the womb and the tomb; a source of inspiration and knowledge; femininity is all its aspects; transition; rejuvenation; sustenance; and traditional Witchcraft.

The most famous story related to Cerridwen is that of the birth of Taliesin, the most well known Celtic prophet and Bard. Cerridwen originally had two children with her husband Tegid Foel. The first child was the beautiful daughter called Creirwy, and the second a misshapen son named Afagddu (*utter darkness*) or Morfran (*great crow*). In an attempt to bring blessings to her unfortunate son, Cerridwen set about creating a potion of inspiration and transformation in her cauldron and set to task a blind man to stir it all year. She also employed a young serving boy called Gwion to fetch wood for the fire and keep the cauldron boiling, but the lad was clumsy and knocked the cauldron while stoking the fire. Three drops of the potion fell onto Gwion's finger and when he placed his finger in his mouth to soothe the burn the power of Cerridwen's potion was imparted unto him.

In a rage that this serving boy had taken the benefits of a potion meant for her son, Cerridwen chased Gwion away. A magical chase ensued, with both Gwion and Cerridwen shapeshifting in order to outwit each other. First Gwion was a hare and Cerridwen the hound; then a fish and an otter; a sparrow and a hawk. Finally Gwion hid himself as one grain of wheat in a field of wheat, but Cerridwen transformed herself into a white hen and devoured all the harvest, in the process devouring Gwion himself. Nine months later she gave birth to Taliesin, the product of love, rage, inspiration and transformation.

Cerridwen is portrayed as our wise grandmother, one who has loved and grieved, gained and lost, blessed and banished, and has taken the experience of her life into the realms of magic. She is a lady of the moon, a keeper of secrets and a wise woman of both earth and sea. A wonderful guide, although sometimes a little difficult, Cerridwen is the Goddess to invoke when life feels overwhelming. She will always answer your call with honesty and inspiration – but be prepared to work hard for your solutions, Cerridwen does not hand out magic freely!

Cerridwen Invocation

Of darkest Moon
Of darkest nights
Thou art wisdom
By fire light
In misty woodland
On mountain peak
In deepest cavern
Knowledge to seek
In Womb
In Tomb
In afterlife
In Love
In Loss
In joy and strife
Of manifestation
Of transformation
Old Crone midwife
Grandmother weaver
Storyteller and seeker
Wisdom teacher
Secret keeper
Bearer of the boiling cauldron
I call thee in, Cerridwen

Demeter

Although Demeter is considered a Goddess of Olympian origin, I personally believe that she is much older in essence and is actually a primal earth mother – a harvest mother or corn Goddess who fed humanity from the earliest steps of our agricultural existence. Within mythology she is believed to be wed to

Poseidon, God of the sea, which is a partnership of both land and ocean. Their daughter was named Kore the maiden (pronounced *Cor-Ray*); although in popular mythology she is better known as the divinely similar and often associated maiden Persephone.

Demeter's association with the seasons is revealed within the story of her daughter's abduction by Hades, Lord of the Dead. As a young maiden Persephone was collecting flowers when Hades fell in love with her and whisked her away on his chariot into the land of the dead. At a loss as to where her daughter had vanished to, Demeter fell into a great despair and searched the world for her. As she grieved, all the harvests failed, the plants died and no new seed would sprout. Fearing for the future of the human race, the Olympian Gods sent Hermes to beg Demeter to release her grief and allow the crops to grow again. Demeter refused to oblige until her daughter was returned, and it was left to Zeus, father of the Gods, to resolve the situation. On discovering that his brother Hades was behind Persephone's disappearance, Zeus sought to make a compromise. Persephone would forevermore spend nine months of the year with her mother in the land of the living, and three months of the year in the land of the dead as Hades' bride. Once reunited with her daughter, Demeter joyfully returned the land to fertility and all the flowers bloomed in response to her happiness. However, Demeter is aware that every year she must allow Hades to take her daughter and in response to her grief the plants and crops die away and the land remains cold and barren until Persephone returns. In this way Demeter is the personification of the earthly seasons, but more than this she is our connection to our internal metaphysical seasons – our emotional wax and wane.

Demeter is the perfect primal mother, and her unconditional love is a testament to the imminence of deity. Invoke or evoke Demeter when you require the balancing and nurturing honesty of a mother, or when you are preparing to reap in your personal harvest. Demeter will also assist those in bereavement with a gentle but empathic outlook.

Demeter Invocation

Belly of harvest,
Walking the cornfields,
Bringer of fruition,
Teacher of the yield
Lover of the world
Mother of the grain
Wise woman of compromise
Wax and Wane
In you we feel
The Wheel of the Year
The season reflecting
Your laughter and tears
In joy we live in abundance
In grief we are bereft
The sun shines for your smile
Then only ice is left
Waiting in the barren
For your blessing of your womb
The gift of fertility
Returning from the tomb
Giving without end
Blessing scattered seed
Reaping in the harvest
Living without need
You are Queen of the lands
As far as eye can see
True Earth Mother
Wed unto the sea
Grant us your blessings
Make home our sacred space
Step into our Priestess

A Goddess with human face

Diana

The Roman Goddess Diana has a long history of worship, and is revered by many modern Pagans. Much like her Greek counterpart Artemis, she is a Goddess of the hunt, of wild nature and of forests, who later evolved into a lunar deity and a Goddess of fertility and childbirth. Despite being described as a virgin Goddess, Diana is also heralded as the mother of Aradia, the Queen of Witches. She is often visually portrayed as a young mother holding a new born child, and with such an image it is clear to see why many of her temples were rededicated to the Virgin Mary during the Christian conversion. Many modern Witches consider Diana to be the essence of the Divine Mother and she is called upon in a variety of Pagan paths as the ultimate Feminine Divine in all her forms.

Diana Evocation

Blessed Diana
Goddess of the crescent moon
Huntress of the forests
Most lovely maiden and mother
I lift my arms towards thee
And raise my voice in praise
Be with me on this moonlit night
Be with me in this sacred rite
Blessed Diana
I welcome thee

Epona

Fair maiden Epona is the protector of horses, a Goddess of fertility, and a holder of the keys to the land of dreams. Unusual for a Celtic deity, her worship was also widespread throughout Roman culture. She is a gentle soul, and offers comfort and blessing to all who follow her. Epona also offers support to the dying, and assistance to the dead by accompanying them into the underworld. This shows the duality of her nature as both a Goddess of fertility and life, and of death and dying. Epona's gentle nature can soothe a soul in grief, and is a wonderful Goddess to call upon in times of bereavement. As the Divine Mare, her function as protector of horses, mules and donkeys makes her a well-loved deity in rural communities.

Epona Evocation

Blessed Goddess of the white mare
Run as wind across green valley
Run as cloud across blue sky
Run as water down the mountains
Run here, run free
I welcome thee
I seek your presence this day
To be with me in my sacred rites
I sing your name in honored tongue
Epona
Epona
Epona
I call thee home

Ereshkigal

Very little written documentation survives about the Mesopotamian Goddess Ereshkigal, Queen of the Underworld, but despite this she still has a deeply devoted following of Pagan Priests and Priestesses in modern days. In Sumerian mythology she is described as the elder sister of the more widely known Inanna or Ishtar, and one of the few remaining myths describing Ereshkigal is the tale of Inanna's journey into the underworld. The land of the dead, also known as Irkalla, is solely Ereshkigal's domain where her word is law and judgment above and beyond any other deity. Ereshkigal is a strong, quiet deity of deep wisdom. When she speaks, her truth is often terrible in its honesty. She sees the best and worst of all, naked in soul and intent.

I include Ereshkigal in these pages to personally honor a deity that I have worked with on many occasions. Ereshkigal, like Brigid and Lugh, came to me without my conscious desire to seek her out. She has offered me strength and wisdom in times of darkness and grief, and through her I have come to better understand the cycles of death and rebirth, the nature of grief and bereavement, and the power of owning one's darkness. She is my Dark Lady, my darkness, and I am blessed by her touch.

Ereshkigal Evocation

Dark Lady
I am honor bound to thy gaze
To thy language of silence and secrets
To thy will of stone and dreadful mercy
I am but a child
No fear of death or cold embrace
Following a dark Angel
Down into the land of dreams
Dark Queen
I call to thee
To stand by your side
Long before I seek the comfort of your kiss
Speak to me of secrets
Of terrible truths
I await your whispered wisdom

Fortuna

Fortuna is the Roman Goddess of fate and fortune, and the personification of Lady Luck. She represents the turning wheel of the seasons and the turning tides, any cycle that shifts from abundance and prosperity to loss and absence. Fortuna is often portrayed as blind or blindfolded, to display her indifference to the fortunes of man based upon their character. She is the deity of good luck and bad, prosperous fortune, and devastating fate. Her associations with abundance also reveal an older aspect as a fertility Goddess, a deity that inspires irresistibility in women.

Fortuna Evocation

Turn your gaze to my voice
Hear my desire for your presence
Look upon me favorably
As I hold you in reverence
You turn the tides
Twist the fortunes of men
Pull down empires
And build them up again
With turn of wheel
With kiss of fate
The chance of us all
Our fortunes to make
With cut of cord
With closure of eyes
The bender of time
To start and end lives
Lady of luck
Hear now my plea
Turn time and tides
In favor of me
Speak to my heart
Whisper in my mind
Step into my life
For my fortunes to find

Freya

A fertility Goddess found in Norse, Germanic and Anglo-Saxon mythology, Freya is one of the most revered of all the Nordic Goddesses. Her strength and passion still speaks to women all over the world, especially those seeking to rediscover independence and strength after patriarchal influence, oppression, or the social devaluing of women's abilities. Not only is she sensual, sexual and unbridled in passion, she is also a fierce warrior and leader of the Valkyries. On the battlefield she gathers souls of the bravest warriors, many of whom she offers an afterlife in her home of perpetual rest. The others she comforts and eases their transition into the halls of Valhalla.

Freya Invocation

Bright Lady and Shaman
Maiden of the Nordic lights
Leader of the wild women
Bringer of new life
Primal in skin bare
Run as wind across the fields
Roaring with passion
Bearing sword to wield
All will part for thee
A warrior of such beauty
Holding all in awe
In fear, in love, in mystery
Shape shifting mother
Always wisdom imparting
Foretelling your children
Ancient skills of crafting
To take form without form
To heal with the hands
To tell of great prophesy
And bring fertility to the land

To speak in animal tongue
To make fire from ice
To soar with the falcon
To make sacred love and life
Beloved Bride
Moon of the cold seas
Be with me now
Gift me with your qualities

Gaia

Gaia is the primordial Earth Mother, the essence of all. In Greek mythology she is the first being to emerge from the time of chaos, and it is by her will that the universe was created and fell into order. She gave birth to planets, to Gods, to Titans, and through her humankind came into existence. Gaia is often perceived in modern Pagan mythology as the living, breathing earth, the conscious Divine energy of the planet on which we live.

Gaia Invocation

Earth Mother
Primal Mother
Giver of life
To man and God alike
Harvest bringer
Wind singer
Earth shaker
Wave maker
Warming fire
To lift the hearts of men higher
Compassion teacher
Balance seeker
Bountiful
Beautiful
Open hearted

For both living and departed
Volcanic soul
Separate and whole
Tide turner
Wild fire burner
Blazing fury
As a warning for all to see
Gaia of compassion and rage
I welcome you
Honor you
Mother of all
Heed me now

Hecate

Hecate is known as a Goddess of the Greek pantheon, but is considered to be originally Thracian or even older. She is a Dark Goddess, a deity of the Moon, of the thresholds, of the underworld and of magic. A triple deity, Hecate is seen as maiden, mother and crone; as the three faces of truth; as the three women of wisdom; and as an entity with the faces of a horse, a dog and a bear. Much like Herne, she is a leader of the night-time Wild Hunt, escorted by packs of baying hounds. She is a shape shifting, wisdom wielding deity of darkness and light, showing us the way to illumination through darkness. Hecate has a prominent following within modern Paganism and Witchcraft, and is often called upon as the Goddess of Witchcraft.

Hecate Evocation

Hail Hecate!
Lady of midnight and magic
Queen of darkness
And light within darkness
Hail Hecate!
Goddess of truth and wisdom

Goddess of secrets
And Divine mysteries
Hail Hecate!
Queen of the crossroads
Mistress of the underworld
Goddess of the threshold
Hail Hecate!
Dark Mother of Witches
In all your forms
We call to thee
Hear us now
Be with us on this moonlit night
Be welcomed to our sacred rite
Hail Hecate!
Hail Hecate!
Hail Hecate!

Isis

Goddess Isis is one of the most well recognized and revered deities of the Egyptian pantheon, and is celebrated by contemporary Pagans from many different paths. She is seen as a supreme mother archetype, a Goddess of birth and rebirth, the mother of Horus, of every Pharaoh, and of Egypt itself. Her power and influence spread far beyond the boundaries of Egypt, into cults all across Europe. The image of Isis breastfeeding Horus has even been associated with the Virgin Mary and baby Jesus.

Isis is also a Goddess of death, medicine and magic, said to have taught early man the science and magic of healing. She is a powerful, intelligent, and challenging mother, incorporating so many diverse feminine attributes that she appeals to a broad array of women from all over the world as a symbol of strength and nurturing.

Isis Evocation

Great Goddess Isis, Mother of all
We cry out to you our beloved Divine
From space without form,
Time beyond time
With our power born of thine
Great Goddess Isis, Queen of Night
Lady of Magic and Mystery
Share your wisdom
With your children
We gather here to honor thee
Great Goddess Isis, Lady of Moon
Daughter of Sky and Mother of Light
Blessed be those
Who call you their own
Who seek the gaze of your sacred sight
Great Goddess Isis, throne of power
Strength and wisdom bound with grace
Daughter of Earth
Queen of rebirth
We welcome you to this sacred space
Beloved Isis spread your wings
Shelter us with your blessings
Queen of Heaven
Hear your children
Isis
Isis
Isis

The Morrighan

The Morrigan, Morrighan, or Mor-rioghain, is an Irish triple-aspect deity, although more often referred to in ancient texts as a queen rather than a Goddess. Although many see The Morrighan as a warrior Goddess, she is so much more than this. She carries a sense of sovereignty, and a leadership over the land and the wellbeing of its people. Her symbols – the wolf, the crow and the cow – show a strong connection to the sky and the land, linking her to the complex cycles of life, death and rebirth. She is the washer in the ford, the foreboder of death, the guide of departed souls, and nurturer of the dead. She is also the wise counsel, the protector, the blessed Queen, and the whisper of knowledge upon the winds.

Morrighan Invocation

Hail to thee
Queen of blood-soaked battlefield
Of fight
Of flight
Of dark-winged messenger
Sovereign Goddess of battle cries
Of clan
Of tribe
Of standing bloody but unbowed
Great Queen of crow
Of wild wolf
Of sacred calf
Of healing wounds with blood and milk
Phantom Queen of sisters three
Macha
Badb
Nemain
I call your names
I seek your blessings in challenges to come
I seek your blessings for fertile lands
I seek your blessings of strength and protection
I seek thee out
To stand by your side
Morrighan

Goddess of my battle cry
Morrighan
Hear me now my Queen

Invoking and Evoking Deity:
Masculine Divine

Everything is dual; everything has poles; everything has its pair of
opposites; like and unlike are the same; opposites are identical in
nature, but different in degree; extremes meet; all truths are but half-
truths; all paradoxes may be reconciled.
— *The Kybalion*

The God resides in all of us, just as the Goddess does. They are
one and the same, both a part of the Divine All, and yet both
opposites in nature. God and Goddess are the extreme degrees of
masculine and feminine upon the same spectrum of Divinity.
Each one of us, as humans, also contain masculine and feminine
qualities to varying degrees, some more than others. As much as
I believe in the social equality of men and women, I also accept,
respect and enjoy the differences between men and women. The
God and Goddess offer the same concept of both equality and
diversity. The God is a very different energy from the Goddess,
unique and potent in masculinity, and yet is the same energetic
Divine All as the Goddess.

For many new to the concept of Divine balance, duality and
polarity, it can be very challenging to connect with the Divine
aspect opposite to your own physical gender. As a woman, I do
find it easier to connect with the Feminine Divine, but that does
not exclude the Masculine Divine from my daily life, spiritual
learning or ritual practice. I too am a part of the Divine All, and
as a woman the Masculine Divine, the God, the Lord, resides
within me.

Invoking or evoking deity is not reserved to the role of a corre-
sponding physical gender, as a woman I am just as capable of
invoking the God and connecting with the Masculine Divine
aspects both within myself and external to myself. If you are

male, know that you are more than capable of reaching out and connecting with the Feminine Divine. However, having the capability of Divine connection and having the skill and wisdom to connect with the Divine are very different things. One should practice connection and communion with both Masculine and Feminine Divine on a regular basis, particularly if you struggle with either end of the spectrum. By understanding your personal connection with the Masculine and Feminine Divine, you will better understand your own masculine and feminine traits.

The God takes many forms, young and old, wild and restrained. He is the Hunter, the Holly King, the Oak King, the Lord of Shadows and the Lord of Light. He is the young Squire, the devoted Knight, the learned Priest and the wise old Sage. He is the God of love and sex, fertility, virility, death and decay. He is the God of honor, justice, retribution, battle, balance, and sacrifice. He is the strength of spirit, the promise of summer, the Green Man of wild woods and farmers' fields. He is the primal urging, and the reasoned scholar. He is the light and the dark, the sun and the shadow, the deep earth and the expansive sky. He resides within every boy becoming a man, and every man facing his death. He is warrior, protector, father and son. He is love and anger, hope and despair, joy and sorrow, creation and destruction. The God is an aspect of the Divine All within our cosmos and within us all.

Charge of the God

Hear my words upon the winds of winter
And subtle summer breeze
Hear my words of truth when you turn towards me
I am the times of change, the cycle of sun
The blessings of bounty and battles won
I am the voice of dissent, of counsel and reason
The hardworking hand of hurt and healing
I am dark and light, day and night,

Harvest and sacrifice
I am cold death and blessed rebirth
The Lord of Shadows and the Green Man of earth
I am the rebelliousness of youth
The wisdom of old age
I am Squire, Knight, Priest and Sage

Seek and you shall find me
For I am within all things, at all times, in many ways
From times passed to future days
I am within each life born
Within each death transformed
Within the very reflection of your gaze
Raise your eyes
For I reside
Within your soul
Call to me and I shall come home
For I am within all things, at all times, in many ways

Calling the God

We all come from the Green God
And to him we shall return
Within the woodland creatures
And the winter fires burn
We ask that you now join with us
Impart your life philosophy
The heat and the hunter rise up
Within the Priest that speaks for thee

Calling the God

Beloved Lord, our Masculine Divine
We ask you here at this time outside of time
To a place of trust and love between
All that is and is yet unseen

Pause a while with us during this rite
Bless us with your wisdom and watchful sight
May the heat and the hunter now coarse through
This humble Priest that speaks for you
Hail and welcome

Calling the God at Samhain

Dark Lord, wild Hunter of the untamed places,
We welcome you into our hearts and homes.
You bless us in the winter months, and reveal the bounty of
life to be found in the harshest of seasons.
With your wisdom to guide us, we seek understanding of our
own wild nature.
With your wisdom to guide us, we seek to reveal the ebb and
flow of energetic journeys.
With your wisdom to guide us, we seek strength, compassion,
and Divine connection for even the darkest of days and
nights.
Horned Hunter, seed of the New Sun, be with us now as we
usher in the new year.

Adonis

Beloved Adonis, the Greek God of desire, is the archetype of
male youth and beauty. He holds sway with many Goddesses,
and is a favorite aspect of divinity for young women discovering
their sexuality. His mythology contains much duality, for his
stories also reveal themes of jealousy, rage, death and rebirth.
Even as a baby, his beauty caused infatuation and possessiveness
leading to an intervention from Zeus, and resulted in Persephone
and Aphrodite alternately spending time with Adonis
throughout the year. This division of time is often related to the
cycle of seasons, and consequently Adonis is seen as a God of
vegetation. Killed in the height of his beauty, Adonis has become
the forever youthful God whose blood spills upon the fields and

invokes new life and beauty from grief and death.

Adonis Evocation

Beloved Adonis
Beautiful and bountiful
Forever sacrificed at the height of life
God of cycles, love and strife
Hear us now as we call to thee
Teach us the wisdom revealed
In blood spilled upon fertile field
Hear us now as we call to thee
Share with us how love transforms
Love found within a heart that mourns
Hear us now as we call to thee
Most cherished Divinity
God of the mysteries
Adonis, beloved,
We welcome you home

Apollo

Greek God Apollo is the son of Zeus and Leto, and twin brother to Artemis, although it is said that he is a day younger than his sister. He is a God of multiple talents, medicine, fine arts, eloquence, music and poetry. He is held as the God of the Sun, of light and fertility. Considering his talents and attributes, many call to Apollo as a God of inspiration when starting new projects.

Apollo Evocation

Light of the Sun,
Shine upon me,
Fill my life with joy and poetry
Bring fertile form to all I do
For in your honor I share my truth
In simple ways I practice my arts

The Divine within my hand and heart
Share your wisdom,
Inspiration,
Dedication,
To all forms of art and fertility
Great God of Light
Shine upon me
So mote it be

Cernunnos

Originally from the Celtic pantheon, Cernunnos is a deity now found widespread throughout Pagan paths. Some believe that Herne the Hunter and Cernunnos are the same God, both described as the Horned One or the Horned God and both with the antlers of a stag. Cernunnos is a God of wild, untamed places, of animals, of hunting, of fertility and of prosperity. He is considered the consort of the Earth Mother Goddess, and promotes the sacred union of peace and love when in harmony with the earth. As a form of Green Man, Cernunnos is also a representation of the seasons, cycles, and rise and fall of vegetation. Communing with him helps us to be more in touch with the land, to better understand the connectedness of all life, and to reflect upon the life and death of flora and fauna.

Cernunnos Invocation

Horned One of forest and glen
Of mountain, valley, lake and stream
Of wild winds and howling beast
Of standing stones and twisted trees
We call to thee
We bid you come
At sound of voice
At beat of drum
See the Priest with antlers raised

Giving form to your grace
Be with us and join as one
Great God Cernunnos
Blessed Horned One
Cernunnos!
Cernunnos!
Cernunnos!

The Dagda

The supreme God of the Irish Tuatha De Danann, The Dagda is also known as The Good God, the Red Man of All Knowledge, and the Father of All. He is the Divine father figure, full of strength and wisdom, and a king of abundance, fertility, music and battle.

Evocation of The Dagda

Great Father and Druid
We seek your presence
Red One of all knowledge
We seek your wise counsel
Warrior, leader, lover and king
Hear us now and be with us
We honor you with raised voice
With song and sound
We honor you with food and wine
With feast and fertility
We honor you with strength of soul
With faith and freedom
We honor your kith and kin
With stories and memories
Good God
Bring forth your wisdom
That we may learn from you this night
We welcome you here

To our sacred rite

Dionysus

The Greek and Thracian God Dionysus has a wild and unrestrained reputation. He is a form of Demi-God, born of the God Zeus and the human mother Semele, but he is no less a potent deity. Known as the God of fertility, vegetation and wine, Dionysus is also a deity of the mystery traditions, of spiritual awakening, of liberation, of inhibition, and of wild ecstasy. His rites are known for seemingly wild abandon, sexuality and almost orgasmic frenzy of dance.

As an outsider God and an extensive traveler, Dionysus can reveal to the practitioner the importance of knowing thyself outside social boundaries, understanding our wild and untamed nature. Invoking Dionysus is like drinking too much wine and believing you can remain emotionally calm and responsible, one cannot lose all inhibitions and still meet all the standards of social expectation.

Personally I feel that if you wish to invoke Dionysus as an individual or as a group, you should find a magical practitioner who can support you from a grounded and removed position to ensure that all involved remain safe and supported. Be wild and wonderful, but wise.

Dionysus Invocation

I call upon thee
Loud and vibrant Dionysus
Bull and beast
Wine and feast
God of mystery
Fill me now
Strip me bare from the inside
Show me my wild and untamed nature
Fill me now

Lift the veil of restraint from my eyes
Let me see with a gaze of love and freedom
Fill me now
Let me stand and dance in glory
Let me raise my voice in ecstasy of thee
On this night
For this sacred rite
I host the wild Divine within me
Welcome Dionysus

Freyr

Frey or Freyr is the Norse God of peace, prosperity and fertility. Brother of Freya, he retains the same revered status within the Nordic pantheon as his sister. Sometimes called the Golden God of the North, it is believed that Freyr presides over both the sun and the rain to bring bountiful harvest to the fields. Although skilled in battle as many other Norse deities, he is primarily a God of love who gave away his prized sword in honor of his love for Gerda. He teaches love in all its forms, from sexuality and fertility, to the honoring of the land and all its creatures. Freyr asks us to work with love, to harvest with love, and to treat all living beings with respect.

Akin to other fertility and vegetation deities, Freyr is also a teacher of sacrifice. Every year at the first harvest he is struck down to bleed out upon the fields and strengthen the harvest, dying every year and born anew after each sacrifice.

Freyr Evocation

Hail good God Freyr!
Lord of the fields
Lord of the earth
Lord of the Vanir
Lord of the heart
We call to thee

We honor thee
With every harvest
Every act of love
Every act of sacrifice
Every act of honest work
We call to thee
We honor thee
Golden God of boars and beasts
Of every hoof and horn
Good God of love and peace
Of forest and field of corn
We call to thee
We honor thee
Hail Freyr
Lord of light and life

Herne

Herne the Hunter, sometimes called Cerne, was often perceived as a local God for Windsor Forest, Berkshire, in England, and as a local interpretation of the Celtic Horned God Cernunnos. However, if he ever was localized to one region, his reach within modern Paganism now extends far beyond that and he is a common deity to invoke when connecting with the Masculine Divine. A green God of forests, fields, and hunting, Herne is portrayed as a wild man with the antlers of a great stag. He leads the Wild Hunt upon a black horse, accompanied by large hounds with red eyes.

Call upon Herne the Hunter as the wild aspect of nature, as the man who remains true to his heart even in the face of adversity, and as potent fertility found within nature even in the depths of winter. Herne may be called by blowing a hunting horn three times at dawn or dusk.

Herne Evocation

Horned One
Hunter of the forests green
We call you here
To rest a while in good company
Pause your hunt
Steady your stead
Rest your hounds
We hail thee
Green God of plenty
God of hunt and howling beast
God of woodland
God of field, forest and stream
We hail thee
And welcome your presence by our fire
All Hail Herne the Hunter!

Lugh

Lugh is a highly revered Celtic deity, not only known for his wide array of talents but also for his wisdom. Although not perceived of as a war deity, Lugh is portrayed as a skilled warrior bearing a spear so bloodthirsty that it would take to battle by itself, tearing through enemies with lightning strikes and fire.

In many modern Pagan paths Lugh is viewed as a Sun God, but historically it is more appropriate to associate him with the power of fire, lightning and storms. Despite being destructive elements, these are all high energy elements of transformation, change and creativity.

Lugh is also a smith and as such is seen as transformational, but it is the kind of transformation won through hard work, perseverance and education. He is vibrant, energetic, honest and enthusiastic, and is an inspiring deity to work with.

Lugh Invocation

Father of Justice,
Both farmhand and leader,
Craftsman and gamesman,
Archer and healer,
Thou art God among men
And the cries in the corn,
The teacher of sacrifice
Forever reborn,
In the Wheel's turn
In the fire's burn,
The giver of balance and love
Both below and above
I am your contender
But thou art the Game
I am in You, You are in me
We are one and the same.

Lugh Evocation

Lugh Ildana
God of many skills
Carpenter and healer
Wordsmith and leader
Music maker
Fire blazer

Lugh Lamfada
Lugh of the long arm
Your fiery spear a lightning strike
Seeking enemy with bright light
Fierce as the blazing sun
Hero hailed battle won

Gift us with your wild wisdom

Your presence lighting our hearts
Teach us the ways of sacrifice
As we walk upon your path

Mabon

Mabon is the little known Welsh deity for whom one of the
Sabbats is commonly named. Best known for his reflection of the
harvest season, the waning light and the rebirth of the sun,
Mabon's mythology is the tale of a child stolen from his mother
Modron (Great Earth Mother) who grieves until he is returned.

The mythology bears similarity to the tale of Demeter and
Persephone, and to the many Gods of sacrifice who die each
harvest until the rebirth of the sun, but his tale is one of youth
and innocence. He is a child of promise. Not much is known
beyond this tale of kidnapping and reunion, but we can tell from
this story and the other characters that play a part within it – the
stag, the blackbird, the eagle, the salmon, and the owl – that
Mabon is associated with the fertility of the land, the strength of
the sun, the wisdom of nature and the cycle of life.

Mabon Evocation

Blessed Mabon
Sweet Child of Summer's End
We call to thee with the song of blackbirds
And the cry of the eagle
With the stamping of hoof
And the splash of the salmon
Through owl's eyes we seek you out
And call you home
Little Lord of Sun
Be with us now
As the promise of all to come
Sweet Divine
We call you home

Odin

The Norse God Odin, Lord of Asgard, King of the Aesir, is one of the most recognized deities in the Norse Pantheon. Odin is a complex and fascinating deity. A God of war and leader of the warrior aristocracy, Odin is also a God of fertility, poetry and wisdom. Odin gave an eye to his uncle Mimir, the God of prophecy and wisdom, in order to drink the sacred waters from the well of wisdom that springs from the root of Yggdrasill. Odin also hung from the world tree for nine days, where he learned nine powerful songs and the wisdom of the runes.

Odin is a deity that demands one to have honor, respect and a willingness to both work hard and sacrifice our comfort to achieve the change and knowledge we desire. He is known as Alfadhir (All-Father), and like many strong, wise but challenging fathers, Odin encourages our personal development by leading with example.

Odin Evocation

Hail Odin!
Bloodied victorious
Lord of Asgard
Wisdom of the Gods
Sound of the runes
He who traded sight for insight
He who sacrificed for knowledge
He who leads the wild hunt
He who demands the virtues
Hear us
The voices of your clan
We call to you
Seek your counsel and your strength
Honor us with your presence
As we honor you this night
Be with your blood, your kith, your kin

Find comfort in our company
Merriment in our halls
Reverence in our rites
Odin, All Father,
Hear our voices
Be welcomed here
Hail Odin!
Hail Odin!
Hail Odin!

Devotionals and Offerings

Many Witches practice daily devotionals or present daily offerings to their deities as a part of their spiritual life. This is a way to honor the deity present in your life, maintain and strengthen your connection to the Divine All, and create a spiritual practice that centers and grounds you at the beginning of each day. It is less common to see a devotion or offering made after invoking or evoking a deity during a ritual, but I do feel that this is good practice in many situations.

When I invoke the masculine and feminine aspects of the Divine All, I do so by connecting to the thread of Divinity that runs through all things, that resides in all things, that exists within the circle participants and within myself. I reach into that spectrum of energy and I call it forth, pulling it from the subconscious to the conscious and giving it form and voice. Many practitioners refer to this energy in generic terms of God and Goddess or Lord and Lady. When I invoke a specific God or Goddess, I am calling to an archetype or an aspect of the Divine All that is both a part of the All and is a separate and distinct entity; an entity with a name, with history, with personality. I am essentially inviting a presence into my home, be that my ritual circle or into my body. The polite thing to do would be to allow my guest to get settled, rather than insisting they start work as soon as they walk through the door. A period of devotional practice, or an offering to the invoked deity, is akin to offering your guest a drink and making sure they are comfortable within your home. It is a small and simple gesture that gives a measure of time to each participant's comfort, be that the God or Goddess invoked, the Priest or Priestess providing the physical host, or the members of the circle adjusting to the presence of the Divine.

Devotionals and offerings do not need to be complex affairs, they can simply be a spoken gratitude at the presence of the God or Goddess, or an offering of food or drink. Many deities enjoy tactile items and pleasant aromas as well as the offering of food and drink. Some practitioners will perform a "cakes and ale" rite at this point in the ritual, but it is more common to see this towards the end of the ritual, after the main reason for celebration or magical workings are completed. A cakes and ale rite can be a blessing bestowed by the Gods, an acknowledgement and sharing of the bounty received in life, a way to consume some of the energy raised within ritual, or a method of grounding participants after energy work. Eating and drinking is a very physical act and can do wonders for bringing participants fully back into their bodies, especially for those who find it challenging to ground any excess energy. However, a devotional offering should not be confused with this part of ritual, as they are two very different concepts.

If you feel it is appropriate to offer an invoked deity a form of devotional or offering of food, wine or gifts, please consider this prior to your ritual and include something you believe will honor or please your chosen deity. You may wish to include each participant in the devotional, or you may wish to keep it simple and choose one member of your group to make an offering on behalf of all the participants. Whatever you choose to do, or not do, be conscious of the comfort and wellbeing of your deity as an honored guest within your sacred rite.

Simple Gratitude
We welcome [the God/dess] into our circle this night. We thank you for your presence. Please accept this gift as a token of our gratitude.

A Welcome
Blessed be the Divine!
For you a gift, a taste of wine
A chance to rest and be at ease

Within this sacred sanctuary
Welcome!

With Love

Great [God], Beloved [Goddess]
Tonight you grace us with your presence
You are the embodiment of the Divine
A Divinity that touches the lives of each person here
From every heart within this circle
We offer you our love
Blessed be

Sabbat and Esbat Inspiration and Prose

Inspiration for celebrations and magical workings can be found everywhere, from classical poetry to modern song lyrics. If something resonates with you, evokes certain memories or raises emotions, then explore how you can adapt these pieces into your rituals.

Remember that ritual language is all about energy, and when you are working solitary you can tailor everything to create the maximum energetic impact. When you are working with others you need to consider how the language you use and the form that it takes will affect the other circle participants. You can adapt poetry or songs into chants to raise energy, or create unique invocations. You can design guided meditations, or use poetry and prose specifically to create a reflective mindset prior to divination. You can use poetry, prose and song to celebrate the seasons, mark a life transition, as a blessing or as a focus for directing energy. Language is only limited by our imagination, and the beginning of any magical undertaking is simply determined imagination.

The following selection of poetry and prose is all designed to reflect, inspire or work with the seasonal cycle, solar cycle or lunar cycle. Please use or adapt these as they inspire you within your own rituals, celebrations and magical endeavors.

Hail Moon
Hail Mistress of the Moon
Slender Virgin of New Light
Bountiful Mother of Blessing
Dark Crone of Deepest Wisdom

Hail to Goddess of Changing Form
Cutting the sky with silver sickle

Turning bright face upon us
The tides chasing at your heel

Hail to the Moon of Many Faces
Moon of tides, Moon of phases
Gaze upon me in benevolent love
As I gaze upon you in timeless wonder

Listening

She smiles at me
And in her eye I see
All the things she would say to me
If she but only had the words
Then again I am aware
Whenever I feel her near
That it is I who needs to hear
The stories I never heard
I raise my eyes
And seek her sight
And bathe within her soft light
To ease my troubled soul
I wax and wane
She does the same
And together we play the game
Of phases to become whole

The Pulling

I stood under the not quite full Moon
And looked up at the slightly obscured stars
I felt like I had been going nowhere
But I knew that I had come far
My feet were sore and my heart heavy
But the pulling still tugged at my belly
I followed my umbilical cord

Back to the beginning of never
I wondered if I would be reborn
Or would I be pulled forever
It occurred to me then that I was paused...
Maybe this is what they mean by choice

Yule

Hail to the God of Yule
Hail to the strong returning Sun
The Holly King no longer reigns
The Oak King's reign has begun!

Midwinter Blessings

In the darkest of winter
In the depths of cold
We are reminded of the sun
And the bounty it holds
In times of hardship
May the blessings bestow
From kith and kin
And strangers unknown
We share and feast
And celebrate
For winter's grasp
Starts to shake
Soon the thaw
Will flood the streams
The ground will soften
The gales will ease
Like sleepy plants
New life begun
We turn our eyes
Towards the growing sun

Winter

The color leeches from the land
The lake still and silent lies
The stag mourns within the forest
Birds call lonely to grey skies
Breath freezes in the air
Hearts melt to see the sun
Walking into wilderness
Winter has begun

Holy Tree

Holly tree, the holy tree
The jewel of winter's crown
Casting blood-bright berries
To the white of winter's gown

Holly tree, the holy tree
Green splendor, blossom white
Harsh reminder of new life
In long dark bitter nights

Holly tree, the holy tree
Bright white and red and green
You are winter's lonely comfort
Eternal living evergreen

Winter's Oak

Great father of the forest
Old king of battles won
Bare branches like stag's antlers
Framing winter's new-born sun
In absence of splendid greenery
Naked to ice and snow
Bear witness to God's fertility

In white-berried mistletoe

Holly King and Oak King (adapted from traditional)
The Holly and the Oak
When they are both full grown
The Oak King fights the Holly King
Upon Midwinter's morn

The Oak King slays the Holly King
And reigns for half a year
The Holly King rises again
When winter's breath draws near

The Holly King lays challenge
Upon Midsummer's day
Holly King slays Oak King
And bears the crown away

When the sun comes round again
At waxing of the year
The Oak King rises up once more
For his time of reign draws near

Hail Sun
Hail to the sun of seasons
Striding bold across the father's skies
Hail to the sun of illumination
Banishing darkness on land and in mind
Hail to the sun of gentle touch
Shadows fleeing before your reaching rays
Hail to the sun of blessing
The kiss of the Divine on my upturned face

Imbolc

Deep in the belly of the earth life now stirs
Awakening within and shaking free of ice and snow
The Goddess carries the child of promise within her arms
Trailing light and warmth wherever he goes
Slowly the world awakens from its slumber
Pushing shadows back from long cold night
All around
Life abounds
Reaching out towards the growing light

Imbolc Festival of Light

Welcome to the festival of light
Where springtime lies within our sight
Earth softens and milk flows
Babies are born, seeds are sown
Soon the thaws will flood the streams
And winter becomes the land of dreams
The Crone returns to the land of snow
And all around us light now grows
Hold high your flame, shine your light
Chase back the shadows and shrinking night
Prepare the path for spring to come
And rejoice now in the growing sun!

Song of Spring

I shake and wake from long slumber
Bones creaking and cracking
Like the sudden snapping of icicles breaking free from the
    bonds of winter
Falling from their perches and transforming in the touch of
    sun
Releasing form
Shivering and shimmering into new wonder

Flowing free and fluid towards new adventure
I release and let the unknown transform me
Unfurling in the promise of light and new life
Full of potential
I awaken, expand and stretch towards the sun
My warming body and soulful sighs adding to the song of
spring

Sacred Union

The heartbeat
Drumbeat
The pulse of earth quickens
The rivers rushing
The oceans heaving
The land bedecked in finery
Calling forth the touch of rain, of sun
Every flower reaching out for sunlight's caress
Turning their faces towards the kiss of sunlight
Every leaf trembling at the whispers of the wind
Fresh green grass wet with dew
The forests filled with the sounds of life
Every creature calling out for a mate
The earth herself awake
Restless
Seeking
Searching
Stretching
Reaching out for her lover
Responding to the touch of light
Chasing back the shadows of winter
And falling in love once again
The earth in throes of ecstasy
A sacred union laid bare for all to see
The beloved earth replies

To a love that lights the whole sky

Lughnassadh Song of the God (adapted from a chant by Ann Moura, original Lord of the Dance by Sydney Carter)

Dance, dance, wherever ye may be!
When you dance with the Lord, he will dance with thee
Turn, turn, a circle then ye form!
And the Lord of the Dance is the Lord of the Corn

Down, down, into the earth he'll go!
Giving life to the grain that in the spring we'll sow
He rules the Shadow Lands 'til Yule
When his Sun is reborn and his life renewed!

Harvest Blessing

May the rains sweep gentle across your fields
May the sun warm the land
May every good seed you have planted bear fruit
And late summer find you standing in fields of plenty

Corn and Grain
(from a chant by Ian Corrigan)

Corn and grain, corn and grain,
All that falls shall rise again!
Hoof and horn, hoof and horn,
All that dies shall be reborn!

Autumn

The beauty of my youth is lost
And now I am but swathed in the colors of transition
My last festivity, my bright farewell
Before I drop my masks of changing roles
Before I stand naked to the elements

In truth, bare and honest
A state of vulnerability that gives birth to new strength
A little death and a long rebirth

Autumn Equinox

Blessings of bright Mabon
Of graceful autumn presence
Blessings of balance
Of silver moon and golden sun
Blessings of bounty
Of seeds sown and harvest grown
Blessings of knowledge found
Between summer's kiss and winter's touch
As the circle turns and darkness reigns
Know all that falls shall rise again
For darkness, there is light
For sorrow, there is joy
For grief, there is love
For despair, there is hope
For loss, there is gain
Without one, the other is without meaning
The harvest of Mabon lies in more than home and hearth
Mabon is a harvest of the mind and heart
May the harvest be blessed and bountiful

Remembering Love

I light a candle in the darkness
And think of you my love
The spark within my heart a burning ember
Smoldering
A pain unending
I cup the light within my hands
As I hold the embers in my heart
I cannot let them die out for fear of losing you again

And so I burn in the darkness
My grief the pain of loving

At Samhain

Blessed be the beloved dead
Each soul a blazing light
Chasing back the shadows in my life
Every life that touched mine
A reason to love, to honor, to inspire
Blessed be the beloved dead
For without you I would not be
The woman that stands as I am today
Blessed be those who shared my path
Who hold a place within my heart
I light a candle as darkness grows
And offer you sanctuary within my home
Blessed be the beloved dead
For what is remembered, lives on.

Births, Deaths, Initiations, Life Blessings

We move through the cycles and seasons of our lives, marking each passing and transition as we mark the Wheel of the Year. From the spring of our birth to the winter of our death, every transition is given due recognition. Celebrations are unique to each individual, although common threads will often appear. Blessings, poetry, prose, and prayers that inspire the individual can be incorporated into any unique, personal celebration, whether that be a full ritual or small family gathering. This following section contains heartfelt and inspirational pieces reflecting upon various life rites, that I hope will inspire your own personal celebrations.

Chant for a Safe Birth

Safe and calm
Without harm
Hear my pleas
And birth with ease

Welcome

Welcome to the world little one
Holding fast to memories of heart beat and blood rush
From the living waters of your mother's womb
You now face the bright world around you
We marvel in your presence
Most cherished soul
Be safe and comforted in our arms
As we hold you in our hearts
Be at peace
Be calm
You are safe
You are loved

You are welcomed home

Greetings

Greetings and salutations little one
Most blessed of little souls
Love surrounds, love abounds
Our family is now whole

A Child Once

A child once walked before us, holding hands for security and
    reassurance
Now a woman/man walks in our stead, and the time has come
    to let go
Your time has come to walk unaided into the world
To make decisions based on the experiences of your youth
To accept the consequences of your actions
To take responsibility for your choices
To know that even as you walk into the world of adults
That every adult is still a child forever learning
It is with grief we say farewell to the child that once was
For the time seems to pass too quickly
And it is with joy we greet the woman/man before us
Knowing that we still have many years together as a tribe, as
    a clan, as a family
We are honored to have been the ones chosen to support your
    youth
And we would be honored to support your journey into
    adulthood
This is the last time as a child that we lift you up
And the first time as an adult that we let you go your own
    way
With pride
With blessing
We acknowledge you as a woman/man in your own right

So mote it be

Moon Woman

Like the cycles of the beloved moon, you wax and wane
From the blessings of your mother's womb, to the blessings of
your own womb
The time has come to celebrate your changing body
And the mind that changes with new awareness and
responsibility
As young as you are now, this stage is your first step into the
world of woman
Into the world of the sacred feminine
Your body will take on new cycles now,
New rhythms,
New tides of ebb and flow, wax and wane
As a maiden flourishing, you will need to adjust to the cycle
of your body
And the effects it will have upon the waters of your emotions
This is a time of change
But all things change
It is the way of the world, and the way of woman
As a woman soon to be, we honor you as maidens we once
were
With love and pride
We see you travel along your journey
From child, to maiden, to woman
Blessed be your journey

Muddy Footprints

Mama, when I look back on my life, what will I see?

You will see your journey, and the path you have trod. You
will see the mud that slowed your progress, the stones that
often made your journey uncomfortable, and the grass that
made your feet run, skip and dance with joy.

Mama, whose footprints are those?

Those are the footprints of the many that walked before you, the few that walked beside you, and the family that first placed your feet upon the path.

Mama, why do my footprints appear and disappear?

Oh child, they don't disappear. At first you have no footprints because I carried you. I held you tight with love and walked my path the best way I knew how. After a little while, I placed your feet upon the path and walked ahead of you to make sure it was safe for tiny toes. I picked you up and dusted you down every time you fell. Soon you learned to run and you overtook me often, running ahead and running back. I watched you explore the path ahead of you and the world around you and I learned much about our journey together. Sometimes the journey was hard and overwhelming. We stepped away from the path to take a break, sometimes to breathe, sometimes to cry, sometimes to enjoy the moment, sometimes to see how far we had come. Then, when we were ready, we would take a big leap into the unknown and continue along the path.

Mama, why does the path split into many?

That is the point in your journey when you had to choose your own way. We stood at the crossroads, and I knew that the time had come for you to walk your own path, be strong and walk tall. We built a special place there, somewhere we could find our way back to if we ever needed each other. We built it with our history and experiences, decorated it with love and magic, shaded it with security, and filled it with treasured memories. Then we held each other close, and you turned and placed your feet upon a new path. Sometimes you walked in the footprints of others, sometimes you strayed from the path and got lost, sometimes we found ourselves walking together again for a while, and sometimes you carved your own path, beating your way through the wilderness and leaving a path for others to follow.

Mama, where does the path lead?

Oh child, the path is your own. It leads always into the unknown, and always towards home.

Rite of Passage

There comes a time in every soul's journey

Where they must face the crossroad of choice

Be it a choice that is easy on the heart but difficult to walk the path

Or a path easy to travel, but a choice hard on the heart and mind

These choices mark the stages of our growing and learning

The stages of our development from child to adult, from adult to elder

The transition of nurtured to nurturer, of protected to protector of others

It is such a transition that you now face

A change in your life marked by choice and circumstance

As those who love you, who honor you, who believe in you

We respect your choice and your path

We stand in solidarity as you enter the new phase of your life

We stand at the crossroads with you to mark the start of your new journey

And we honor you for who you were

We honor you for who you are

We honor you for who you have the potential to be

Choose your path and step into the unknown knowing that we support you

Manifest your new life

With our love and blessing

Dedication Prose

Birthed anew I am,

And I feel there is no light in my life
But that which was there in the beginning
And will be there at the end.
The Goddess guides us all
To walk her path
And this day I felt that I have long ago
Placed my feet upon her path
And yet have only walked it in my dreams.
I have pledged myself to thee
Mother of all, and to you the Hunter,
The consort of love and laughter
And safe in this knowledge of re-awakening –
I am born all over again

Irish Marriage Blessing (Adapted from traditional)
May the Divine be with you and bless you
May you see your children's children
May you be poor in misfortunes
and rich in blessings
May you know nothing but happiness
from this day forward

Handfasting Blessing
(Based on a Pagan Blessing by Ed Fitch)
Above you are the stars, below you the stones
As time does pass, remember:
Like a star should your love be constant, even when not on show. Like a stone should your love be firm, yet smooth with the passage of time. Be close, yet not too close, for the cypress will not grow in the shadow of the oak. Possess one another, yet be understanding of each other's freedom. Have patience with one another, for storms will come but they will pass quickly. Be free in giving of affection and warmth. Hold hands often, and be passionate and sensuous to one another.

Have no fear, and let not the ways or the words of others give you unease, for the two of you will support each other, now and always.

Romany Marriage Blessing of Fruit and Wine

The HPS will present the couple with half an apple cut crosswise to reveal the star within.

HPS: As the stars of the sky appear within the fruit of the tree, so you will be the fruit that feeds each other, and the star that guides you home to one another.

Bride and Groom: So we will

The Bride and Groom both take a bite from the apple and replace it on the offering plate.

HPS: As the fruits of the earth are transformed into the drink of celebration, so shall the fruits of your marriage be transformed into many reasons to celebrate.

Bride and Groom: So it shall.

The Bride and Groom both share a drink of wine, cider or mead, then sprinkle a little as libation to Gods and ancestors.

Handfasting Vows I

From this day on I choose my beloved to be my partner and lover for as long as love shall last

To live with you and laugh with you
To stand by your side and sleep in your arms
To be joy to your heart and food to your soul
To be your constant companion and closest friend
To love you and strive to bring out the best in you always
And to be the best that I can be for you

Handfasting Vows II

Each and every day I promise
To hold you in my arms

To grow with you in truth
To laugh with you and to cry with you
To be with you
And to love you with all that I am and all that I shall become
This I promise from the depth of my heart my mind and my soul,
For as long as our love shall last

Apache Marriage Blessing (traditional interpretation)

Now you will feel no rain, for each of you will be shelter for the other. Now you will feel no cold, for each of you will be warmth to the other. Now there will be no loneliness, for each of you will be companion to the other. Now you are two persons, but there is only one life before you. May beauty surround you both in the journey ahead and through all the years. May happiness be your companion and your days together be good and long upon the earth. Treat yourselves and each other with respect, and remind yourselves often of what brought you together. Give the highest priority to the tenderness, gentleness and kindness that your connection deserves. When frustration, difficulties and fear assail your relationship, as they threaten all relationships at one time or another, remember to focus on what is right between you, not only the part which seems wrong. In this way, you can ride out the storms when clouds hide the face of the sun in your lives – remembering that even if you lose sight of it for a moment, the sun is still there. And if each of you takes responsibility for the quality of your life together, it will be marked by abundance and delight.

Handparting Rite (Divorce)

Once we walked the same path, but now that path separates and travels in different directions. We stand at a crossroads and face an uncertain future, but we must be certain of this first step. Today we make the decision to cut the ties that bind us, so that we may both move forward with free will and forgiveness wherever our new paths take us.

Prayer for the Dying (author unknown)

May we walk upon this earth once again
Once again beneath the same blue sky
Then may our lives intertwine
And may we remember, you and I

Prayer of the Dying

Blood of my Blood
Bone of my Bone
I feel the Gods call me home
Heart of my Heart
Kith, Clan and Kin
A new journey now begins
Forgive me
For all the things I cannot do, for all the things left unsaid
I forgive myself
And grant myself freedom within death
As I depart I will be at peace
If you hold me in your hearts and remember me
What is remembered, lives

Last Rites Blessing

The wheel of the world turns, Earth blesses you
The winds of change whisper, Air blesses you
The flame of love burns bright, Fire blesses you
The river flows to the sea, Water blesses you
The Divine calls your name, Spirit blesses you

Death of a Loved One

We gather here today in a circle of love and trust between
All that is seen and yet unseen
To mourn the passing of one who has touched hearts and minds
 To celebrate with joy the wonder of their life
 To hold hands and hearts, hearts and hands
 As united in grief and love we stand
 We bid farewell to a dear soul who journeys far from us
 Leaving physical form and returning to star dust
 We understand the cycle of birth and death
 And know that their energy never ends
 It scatters out into our universe, the dancing spiral
 A part of all that was and remains eternal
 With their love upon us, and our love upon them,
 We know that we must part ways with our dear friend.
 We are touched and forever changed by a life lived so well
 On this day we simply say hail and farewell…

Honoring the Beloved Dead

From the dawn of your first days
To the sunset of your last breath
I honor you
For all the seasons of your soul
Through the wheel of your life
I honor you
For all the lives you touched
And the work you completed
I honor you
From the time you walk through the veil
To the time you walk upon the Earth again
I honor you
May my love surround you
May my thoughts reach you

May you be held in love and honor from this moment
Until the end of time
So mote it be

Various Blessings

There are many blessings and mini rituals that are incorporated into life rites and seasonal celebrations. Some are traditional within many eclectic Wicca and Witchcraft paths, some are common within various Pagan paths, and some have historical significance as prayers and blessings shared within family groups. This chapter includes a variety of new or adapted prayers, blessings and ritual prose that may be included within your own celebrations.

The Great Rite (symbolic)
As the Athame is to the Male,
So the Chalice is to the Female
For what one lacks, the other may give
There is no greater power in the universe than that of love
Blessed be the union

The Great Rite (literal)
(The High Priestess will invoke the Lady, and the High Priest will invoke the Lord. If specific deities are being invoked, please choose your deities wisely. For those needing clarification, The Great Rite is a sexual act and must only be performed between consenting adults with love and trust.)
HPS: I am your Goddess
HP: You are my Goddess
HPS: You are my God
HP: I am your God
HPS: Together as one
HP: United as one
Both: There is no greater power
   Than that of our love
   Blessed be our union

Simple Gratitude

Goddess Divine
Within my heart and mind
I thank you for the blessings bestowed upon me
With gratitude and joy
I offer this simple appreciation

God Divine
Within my heart and mind
I thank you for the blessings bestowed upon me
With gratitude and joy
I offer this simple appreciation

Gratitude (based on a prayer by Scott Cunningham)

What no human ear could hear, you heard
What no human eye could see, you saw
What no human heart could bear, you transformed
What no human hand could do, you did
What no human will could change, you changed
You change everything you touch
And everything you touch changes
I thank you for the transformation of my soul and life
A humble thanks from one who has spoken and been heard

Meal Blessing

Harvested from fertile earth
Blessed with sun and rain
May this soul be nourished
And this body sustained
By the bounty before me
Blessed be

Saxon Cake Day Chant

Cakes for the Lady!

Cakes for the Lord!
Celebrate the Underworld's opening doors!

Bread and Wine Blessing

From the sun to the corn
From the corn to the flour
From the flour to the bread
May we be blessed by this bounty
May we never hunger
We consecrate this bread in the name of the Lord and Lady
Eat and be merry

From the rain to the vine
From the vine to the fruit
From the fruit to the wine
May we be blessed by this bounty
May we never thirst
We consecrate this wine in the name of the Lord and Lady
Drink and be merry

Winter's Bounty Blessing

From skies to the rains,
From the rains to the roots,
From the roots to the fruits,
From the fruits to the wine.
We consecrate and bless this wine in the name of the Lord of
    Shadows, the Dark Goddess, and the beloved dead.
Raise your cup in blessing of our bounty!

From the earth to the seed,
From the seed to the corn,
From the corn to the grain,
From the grain to the bread.
We consecrate and bless this bread in the name of the Lord of

Shadows, the Dark Goddess, and the beloved dead.
Break your bread in blessing of our bounty!

Mead Blessing

From the rain to the flowers
From the flowers to the bees
From the bees to the honey
From the honey to the mead
May we be blessed by this bounty
May we never thirst
We consecrate this mead in the name of the Lord and Lady
Drink and be merry

Prayer of Light

Our Lord and Lady
Thou art everywhere
Blessed be thy names
Thy cities, woodlands and open plains
Be sacred
To all those who walk your path.
Bless us this day
With joy and laughter
And surround us with love and light
As we love those around us
For life is to Cherish
And Love
And Learn
For all our time together
So mote it be

Peace and Love

Peace be with me
Peace surround me
Peace within me

Peace around me
Peace above
Peace below
Peace I am
Peace I know

Love be with me
Love surround me
Love within me
Love around me
Love above
Love below
Love I am
Love I know

Witches' Lorica

Strength be with me
Strength surround me
Strength within me
Strength around me
Strength above
Strength below
Magic I am
Magic I know

Witches' Creed

I am a Witch in mind and heart
I speak my truth and walk my path
I help and heal where there is need
Remain honest in thought and deed
I cherish everything I know
And use each moment to learn and grow
I stand strong for my beliefs
Strive for fairness and equality

I tread lightly upon the Earth
Honor the cycles of death and birth
I respect all forms of Divinity
Found both without and within me
Before my Gods this I swear,
I am a Witch, my truth laid bare

Gaelic Blessing (traditional)

Deep peace of the running wave to you
Deep peace of the flowing air to you
Deep peace of the quiet earth to you
Deep peace of the shining stars to you
Deep peace of the infinite peace to you

Fivefold Kiss

Blessed be my feet that walk the path of the Old Gods
Blessed be my hands that work wonders in the world
Blessed be my mouth that speaks wisdom and truth
Blessed be my eyes that see many perspectives
Blessed be my ears that hear the secrets of the universe

Elemental Kiss

Blessed be my feet that walk barefoot upon the earth
Blessed be my hands that shape and manifest my desires
Blessed be my heart that swells with love and compassion
Blessed be my mouth that gives voice to thought and reason
Blessed be my mind that animates a soul in physical form

Fivefold Kiss II

I call the blessings of the Goddess and God upon me!
Blessed be my feet that walk the path of the God and Goddess
Blessed be my sexuality that honors life
Blessed be my heart that holds love for my path
Blessed be my lips that speak the sacred names

Blessed be my mind that houses knowledge of the ways

The Witch's Rune
(based on the Witch's Rune by Gerald Gardner)

By darkest night
By shining moon
Hearken now to the Witch's Rune
Water and Earth
Air and Fire
Attend me now, aid my desire
By Will and wisdom
Power and blade
I call thee forth, energy raised
By East and West
North and South
Magic within cast about
By powers of moon and sun
As I speak this spell be done
By powers of land and sea
As I Will it, so mote it be

Three Knot Magic

By knot of one, my work begun
By knot of two, my will be true
By knot of three, so mote it be

Three Knot Magic II

The first knot is for who I was
The second is for who I am
And knot three is for who I will be

Nine Knot Magic

By knot of one, my spell has begun
By knot of two, my intent be true

By knot of three, I raise the magic in me
By knot of four, build form from thought
By knot of five, the spell comes alive
By knot of six, all elements mix
By knot of seven, the spell is woven
By knot of eight, I seal the fate
By knot of nine, the wish be mine

Song of the Druid Amergin

I am the wind blowing over the ocean,
I am the wave of the sea,
I am the mummer of the billows,
I am the ox of seven battles,
I am the hawk on the crag,
I am the golden drop of the sun,
I am the fairest of blooms,
I am the wild boar in boast,
I am the salmon in the pool,
I am the lake on the plain,
I am the craft of the poet,
I am the word of knowledge,
I am the spearpoint of battle,
I am the inspirer of man with the fire of thought,
I, alone, know the secret of the stone door.

Celtic Blessing (traditional)

May the road rise up to meet you
May the wind always be at your back
May the sun shine warm upon your face
And the rain fall soft upon your fields

Irish Prayer (traditional)

For every storm, a rainbow
For every tear, a smile

For every care a promise
And a blessing in every trial
For every problem life brings
A faithful friend to share
And for every sigh, a sweet song
And an answer for every prayer

Celtic Blessing of Light (traditional)

May the blessing of light be on you
Light without and light within
May the blessed sunlight shine on you
And warm your heart
Until it glows like a great peat fire

Old Irish Blessing (traditional)

May love and laughter light your days
And warm your heart and home
May good and faithful friends be yours
Wherever you may roam
May peace and plenty bless your world
With joy that long endures
May all life's passing seasons
Bring the best to you and yours

Apache Blessing (traditional interpretation)

May the sun bring you new energy by day,
May the moon softly restore you by night,
May the rain wash away your worries
And the breeze blow new strength into your being,
And all the days of your life may you walk
Gently through the world and know its beauty.

Ancestor Blessing

May the nourishment of the earth be yours

May the fortune of the winds be yours
May the clarity of light be yours
May the fluency of the ocean be yours
May the protection of the ancestors be yours

Descent of Brigid (adapted from traditional)
Brigid, daughter of the Dagda
Brigid, daughter of Danu
Brigid, wife of Bres
Brigid, mother of Ruadhan

Brigid daughter of Dugall the brown,
Son of Aodh,
Son of Art,
Son of Conn,
Son of Crearer,
Son of Cis,
Son of Carmac,
Son of Carruin

Brigid of the mantles
Brigid of the hearth fire
Brigid of the twining hair
Brigid of the omens
Brigid of the white feet
Brigid of the kine
Brigid of the white palms
Brigid of smith craft
Brigid of the sisters three
Brigid of the sacred flame
Brigid, friend of women
Brigid, woman of wisdom

Each day and each night that I say the Descent of Brigid

I shall not be slain
I shall not be wounded
I shall not be imprisoned
I shall not be harmed
I shall not be torn asunder
I shall not be despoiled
I shall not be down-trodden
I shall not be made naked
I shall not be rent
Nor will I be forgotten
No sun shall burn me
No fire shall burn me
No beam shall burn me
No moon shall burn me
No river shall drown me
No brine shall drown me
No flood shall drown me
No water shall drown me

I am under the shielding of good Brigid each day
I am under the shielding of good Brigid each night
I am under the keeping of the exalted one,
Every dawn, every dusk, every dark, every light.
Brigid be my sacred flame
Brigid be my spirit
Brigid be my heart and hands
Brigid be within me
That the power of shaping be with me
That the power of inspiration be with me
That the power of healing be with me
In every realm of kith and kin

Brigid above me
Brigid below me

Brigid around me
Brigid within me
Brigid of my truest heart

Chants to Raise Energy

Many Pagans understand the relationship between chants or mantras and energy. Chants of various forms are used all over the world in many cultures to elicit an emotional or mental response within the practitioner. Some chants change our brainwave patterns, creating deep meditative states. Some chants are designed to embed new concepts or ideas deep into our subconscious. Just as certain songs we hear make us feel uplifted and enlivened or relaxed and sedate, particular chants can also raise or lower our energy levels.

This technique of raising energy is common practice in rituals, often combined with drumming, clapping and dancing. The use of language can play an important part in creating a group mentality for all the participants, as well as raising and directing energy. By harnessing each practitioner's thoughts through a simple uniform pattern of language, the High Priest, High Priestess or group leader can better direct everyone's intent towards a single goal. Chants can be written with a particular outcome in mind, such as a safe birth, or can focus on just raising and releasing the energy.

When working with a large group, I prefer to use a short chant that is simple to say, easy to remember, and works on a quick, repetitive beat. This kind of chant enables a group, even a group new to working together, to build energy slowly and easily. A simple chant allows everyone to participate without the unconscious fear of speaking incorrectly, and a repetitive beat allows for the pace of the chant to increase gradually. The pace of a chant can be increased naturally as participants become more heightened, or can be controlled by the group leader through clapping or drumming. The pace of a chant is usually increased to the point of impossibility, when participants can no longer verbally keep up with the speed of the repetitions. A frenzy of sound or a sudden silence can complete the chant and release the energy raised.

Although it is natural for large groups to increase the pace of a chant when building energy, it is not the only technique. Repetition of a chant or mantra can build energy regardless of the pace used, and in fact some mantras work better on a slow pace. Consider the beauty and grace of Buddhist or Sanskrit mantras. These forms of repetitive chant still build energy and create an altered state of consciousness in the practitioner, but they are slow and gentle. This kind of gentle mantra can be a blessing for a solitary Pagan, or a small group who feel more comfortable without the physical high energy that comes with fast paced chants.

It must also be noted that a fast paced chant can also have the effect of increasing our heart rate, which may not be beneficial to some practitioners. A chant can be spoken slowly to a regular rhythm, or sung quietly over and over until the practitioner feels the building of energy in and around their body. A group using a slow chant may need a clear cue from the group leader to release the energy at the same time, since there is no natural culmination of the chant.

I certainly suggest experimenting with chants and mantras to find what works well for you as an individual and for your regular group or coven. Practice with different types of language, different styles of chants, and different tempos, to observe the energetic effects. When designing a chant, keep these simple rules for magical writing in mind:

W – Words: Consider the words you use, the meaning behind them, the energetic effects of them and the subconscious influence they have.

R – Rhyme, Rhythm and Repetition: Chants, invocations and spells are easier to remember when they rhyme, have energetic impact from the use of repetitive sounds and beats, and work more effectively on the mind when they have a steady rhythm.

I – Intent: Keep in mind the intent and the overall focus of your magical writing. When writing a chant to raise energy, consider whether you wish to include the intended recipient of your released energy as a part of the chant, or whether you want a chant that harnesses a particular idea or concept.

T – Tempo: Consider the pace of your chant, slow or fast, and make sure that it can be repeated easily if the pace is designed to increase. Tempo can have very emotive effects upon the practitioner, but constantly changing tempo can be discordant and disruptive.

E – Energy: Energy underlies everything. The energy of the words you use, the intention you are creating, the method in which you use one form of energy to raise more energy, the energetic results of your written or spoken word. Put energy into your work to receive energy back.

A Selection of Chants

Blessed be the energy,
For I am all, and all is me

To me, through me, I call thee in,
To me, through me, Form within,
To me, through me, Power grows,
To me, through me, Power flows…

I cleanse, I cast, I call
Evoke, engage, enthrall

I am power, I am grace
I am spirit with human face

By glowing moon
By shining sun

My power grows
My will be done

Earth Air Fire Water
Harness all, my world to alter

From earth to sky
From land to sea
Power raised to work through me

Around me now the power grows
As above so below
Within me now the power flows
As above so below

Earth my body
Water my blood
Air my breath
Fire my spirit

Raise our voices
Raise our hands
Raise the power from the land

Raise our voices
Stamp our feet
Awaken now the earth that sleeps

Brigid of the sisters three
Burning bright, burn in me

This is the time
This is the hour
Here and now

I raise my power

The Rivers are Flowing
(adapted from a chant by Diane Hildebrand-Hull)
The rivers are flowing
Growing and flowing
The rivers are flowing
Down to the sea
Mother carry me
Your child I will always be
Mother carry me, down to the sea
The hills they are calling
Rising and falling
The hills they are calling
Calling to me
Father run with me
Your child I will always be
Father run with me, wild and free

I am she and she is me
Woman to woman, forever known
I am she and she is me
Maiden, Mistress, Priestess, Crone

I am he and he is me
Man to man, through the ages
I am he and he is me
Squire, Knight, Priest and Sage

Charity Chant
Earth turns
Air knows
Fire burns
Water flows

Grant me wisdom
Grant me aid
Guide my power
As it is raised

Meditations and Journeys

Mind (as well as metals and elements) may be transmuted, from state to state; degree to degree; condition to condition; pole to pole; vibration to vibration. True Hermetic Transmutation is a Mental Art.

— *The Kybalion*

The following collection of poetry, prose, guided meditations and visualizations are designed to inspire your inner journey. Each piece is different and unique, yet easily adaptable to the individual practitioner. They are to be tried and tested, reworded and shaped to fit your inner being, to bring forth the greatest mental, emotional and spiritual responses possible. Some of these words may touch old bruises or itch old scars, do not shy away from that. If you have a deep connection, even an uncomfortable one, with any of the pieces that follow it is worth exploring that connection.

Pagan paths vary, but there is always one constant that continually surfaces – "Know Thyself". Know thyself intimately, know thyself completely. Since we are forever changing, growing and evolving, we can only work to know ourselves from past to present, for our future selves remain unknown. Face the journeys that inspire and uplift you, and face the journeys that make you anxious or insecure. Travel deep into your own psyche and explore your reactions to words and images. Ponder upon the words on these pages, and wonder about your attraction and avoidance of each collection. Put pen to paper and write your own story, one where you know the beginning but have yet to discover the end.

Touching Divine

A God to me
Divine male incarnate
Filling my eyes with potentiality
Narrowing my vision until all that remains is you
Beyond place
Beyond time
Beyond world of flesh or dream
Somewhere in between
I meet you there
You hail me as Goddess
Not unreal, not mythical, but Divine and human
With belly full of baby scars
Eyes surrounded with laughter lines
And hair kissed with winter's touch
Goddess still I am
And it is true to me, in honesty, in beauty
For I am Divine in your eyes
As you are in mine
I raise a hand of time gone by
Brush a hair from your eyes
And touch the wonder of Masculine Divine
My path to God through your heart
Your path to Goddess through mine

Beyond Tomorrow

Within the fire we all become
Ancient man mesmerized
The simple tasks tire the hands
The good life, a hard life
There is no more bartering
Haggling, begging and coaxing
We are beyond the desire for more
No more hoping

Within the water we all become
The reason for living and loving
The fetch water, carry wood
A philosophy of having
There is no more waterfall
Overspill, cascade of emotion
We are beyond the stagnant
Carried away in tidal motion
Within the earth we all become
A nurtured plant with face
Lifted towards the sun
Moving in place
There is no more receiving
Merely sowing and reaping
We are beyond the taking
Storing and heaping
Within the wind we all become
The cry of voices unleashed and free
The wind removes the wool from our eyes
And finally we can see
There is no more forgiving
No more ifs, buts, I wish, I need
We are beyond the arguments
It simply is, and we simply be

Woven

Grandmother spider
Weave me a new web
One I can throw around me
Like a comfort
Cover it in morning dew
Let it sparkle in the sunlight
Let me tangle myself up in my dreams
Attract it all towards me

Fragile and strong
A lifetime long
And only a second of connection

Greet the Day

The cool breeze wraps around me
As I stand to greet the day
The mist skims the tree tops
Green fades to grey
My frustration builds as my view is marred
By trucks and stone and malls
And I long to be encompassed
Nature blurring all
I breathe and focus
My toes tickled by dew on grass
White sky, flying gulls
It is as I ask
Mother Nature holds me close
Even in brick and stone
The flowers push through man's foundation
A resistance of their own
Mother Nature holds me close
Kissing tears away with salty air
Tickling my skin for shivers and smiles
Running wild through my hair
Mother Nature holds me close
Warming flesh with sun's blaze
Invoking thought with stars on velvet sky
Reflective with lunar gaze
Mother Nature holds me close
In arms of tree roots, branch and leaves
In flowers, hedge and crops
In wild unrelenting weeds
Mother Nature holds me close

With tidal river flowing by
And she answers my frustrations
With one almighty cry
I am here
Always
Forever
Still
Walk your path
See me with you
Every step of the way
Look for me
As I look for you
I am here
I am here
Whenever you greet the day

Inner Temple Journey

There is darkness, deep and total. Within the darkness there is subtle sound, soft and gentle, rustling of wind in leaves. Beneath that sound is a quiet, rhythmic, ebb and flow, the gentle sound of sea on shore. As you breathe in the darkness and absorb the gentle sounds, your heart slows and relaxes into the rhythm of the world around you.

(Pause)

You are aware of the breeze upon your skin, warm and salty on your lips. The world feels at peace. Slowly the darkness shifts, lifting through misty grey to rich color, revealing the woodland around you. Beneath your feet the first fall leaves lie on a worn path, twisting through the trees ahead of you. As you walk you enjoy the fresh clear dawn, feeling light and healthy.

(Pause)

The sounds of the sea move closer and the trees become more sparse. Ahead the trees give way to an empty sand beach that stretches in both directions as far as the eye can see. Walking out onto the beach, you feel the coolness of the sand beneath your feet. Fresh air wet with spray from the ocean settles on your skin. Far to the left the land rises, revealing a cliff and cavern network between the woodland and the beach. You turn towards the caves, the sea beside you, lapping at your feet as you walk.

(Pause)

When you reach the cliff, you can clearly see the cave entrance ahead of you. As you step inside, you become aware of three more cave entrances within the rear wall of the cave. Each entrance is blocked by a door.

The first door is made of stone, and covered with cobwebs. This is your past, time been and gone.

The second door is warm wood, hinged with strong wrought iron. This is your present, your here and now.

The third door is sleek metal, smooth and without handle. This door leads to your future, a place of change and possibility.

As you reach out to touch the warm wood of the second door, it silently opens ahead of your stretching fingertips. Inside lies a circular cave of smooth ledges, filled with hundreds of white candles. Everywhere your eyes settle the candles splutter into flame, until every ledge is filled with flickering light. The cave is warm and inviting and you step inside. In the center of the room is a simple wooden bench bathed in the light of the candles. Take a seat here, pause a while, and feel the energy of this place. This cave is your inner sanctuary, your time outside of time, your sacred space outside the physical world.

(Pause)

As you sit here you feel at complete peace with yourself, your journey and the lessons you have learned. In this space your guides may visit you and offer advice for challenges yet to come. Be still here. Be safe in the strength of the stone walls around you, deep in the belly of Mother Earth. Bathe in the warm light of hundreds of flickering flames, warming your skin, making you feel calm and receptive. Listen to the distant sound of sea on shore and feel rocked by its rhythm. This is a protective place of deep meditation, only accessible by you and the guides you invite to enter.

(Long pause)

When you feel ready to leave, pause at the doorway and watch as the candles darken one by one. The door closes behind you with a dull thud and the sharp sound of metal locking into place. Your temple is secure and protected. As you turn towards the beach you can see the sun starting to set over the water, the deep rich pinks and reds tinting barely noticeable clouds. The fresh salt air is enlivening after the warmth and seclusion of your temple. The breeze skips across your skin and makes you feel awake and refreshed. You are relaxed and recharged, ready to journey home.

Walking away from the caves and back towards the woodland will slowly but surely bring you back to conscious awareness and the world around you will fade. Take your first step and feel the sand shift beneath your feet... 10... As you take another step feel the grains of sand blown against your skin by the breeze... 9... Walking along the beach brings you closer to home... 8 Ahead of you the woodland comes closer, leaves rustling, shadows shifting... 7... Turn your back on the ocean and walk towards the woodland... 6... You hear the tidal motion behind you rushing forth and back in eternal rhythm... 5... The beach inclines towards the tree line and you rise slightly as you walk... 4... Stepping under the canopy of the trees changes the light around you to dappled dusk... 3... The path ahead lies in darkness but you know the path is clear and you trust your footing... 2... Stepping into the darkness you place your feet firmly on the worn path, the ground solid beneath your feet... 1... Stand still in the darkness and breathe deeply, inhaling and exhaling the damp scent of earth and leaves... When you are ready, become aware of your physical body. You no longer smell the earth and leaves, instead the room around you offers the scent of home. Be aware of what you can hear. Be aware of your body's position. Release any tension your muscles hold, wiggle your toes, clench and relax your hands, roll your shoulders, turn your head from side to side. You are grounded in the here and now. You are relaxed, calm and re-energized. When you are ready, open your eyes.

Know that this temple lies deep inside your mind, and whenever you need the sanctuary, it will be there for you.

Simple Chakra Meditation

Breathe deeply, eyes closed. Breathe in. Breathe out. As you breathe you notice the sharp scent of cut grass tickling your nose. Breathe in. Breathe out. You stand on manicured lawn, in the fresh bright early morning light. In front of you lies a large hedge maze, the opening surrounded by an arch of red roses climbing a clean white trellis.

(Pause)

Walking towards the arch, the grass is springy beneath your feet giving you a sense of lightness. Feeling like you have a skip in your step you focus on the white archway ahead. You notice that the roses seem to all be in bud, the potential of their beauty evident but not yet revealed. Stand beneath the arch, observe the sparkling dew still shimmering on buds and leaves, and breathe in the soft scent of closed flowers. As you breathe in and out, notice how the flowers seem to shake and shimmer, scattering dew drops around you, and slowly opening their rich red petals. As they turn their faces to the sun, the heady scent of fresh rose fills your being and your body relaxes.

(Pause)

Stepping through the arch, you feel awake and grounded, calm and secure in the path ahead of you. Walk through the maze, trusting your instincts, for you already know the way ahead. The sunlight only reaches so far into the depths of the hedge maze, creating shafts of bright light and pools of cool shadow. Walking through a shaft of light, notice how the warmth caresses your skin and how the light picks out tiny specks of pollen in the air making the sunbeam sparkle around you. Soon you come across another arch of sleeping flowers, this time in deep orange. Reach out towards them and watch as they slowly shake off their slumber and stretch their petals out towards the light. The scent of orange blossom makes you smile to yourself, and you breathe deeply to take in the light fresh fragrance.

(Pause)

When all the flowers have awoken, step under the arch and continue the journey before you. The grass is cool and damp beneath your feet, and a gentle breeze rustles the hedge around you. You notice the leaves on the hedges are not all the same color, some as light as peridot, some as bright as emerald, some the rich dark green of heavy velvet. The whole hedge seems vibrant with color. As you turn another corner, a new arch appears covered in bright yellow buds. A lemon fresh scent reaches you and you feel enlivened and happy. As you eagerly reach forth to wake the flowers, they open suddenly in a cascade of yellows from subtle sunshine to burnished gold.

(Pause)

Happy and confident, you slip under the arch and rush along the path seeking the next arch. As you move swiftly along the path, you walk through shafts of warm sunlight and patches of deep cool shade. Your skin is teased by the changes and goosebumps shiver along your arms. You turn each corner quickly, searching for the next arch of flowers. The archway you find is covered in the strangest green flowers, big broad petals in sparkling emerald hues. The scent is familiar, but almost indistinct, and somehow makes you think of home. Gently you reach out to touch one of the closed buds, and the large flower opens in your hand revealing gossamer thin petals. Slowly, all around you, the flowers open in an act of trust, wavering in the breeze.

(Pause)

Carefully you step under the arch, trying not to damage any flowers as you pass. Deep in thought about the fragility and beauty of the flowers that just opened before you, you continue slowly through the maze. Unexpectedly the next arch appears, covered in tiny bright blue climbing flowers. Many of the buds are already open, and even before you step under the arch many of the tiny buds burst open and eagerly turn towards the light. The scent is sharp and fresh, somehow reminiscent of pines and mountains.

(Pause)

You touch a few tiny flowers as you pass, offering sweet nothings of beauty to their upturned faces. As you walk deep into the maze, you twist and turn along pathways that seem less and less familiar. Pausing, you realize you are no longer sure of your direction. Taking a few hesitant steps forward, you breathe a sigh of relief when you see an arch appear on the path to your left. Walking towards it, you can see it is covered in flowers of deep purple, lilac, and violet. Although it appears to be just one plant, many of the flowers seem different, varying in shape and size. They release a strong heady scent that makes you feel a little overwhelmed and drowsy. One by one they open before you, each flower unique yet somehow connected to the one before. You feel connected and at peace with the world around you, as if each flower that opens connects a part of you to greater whole. Humbled by your place in the cosmos, you contemplate the dance of flowers, of animals, of people, of planets, of the spinning universe around you.

(Pause)

Continue along the path, aware of the interlocking hedges beside you and the grass compressing beneath your footsteps. Soon you reach the center of the maze, the hedges suddenly giving way and revealing a sanctuary of stone and white flowers. In the center is a small stone temple, seven carved pillars rising towards the sky, covered in vines and climbing flowers. A water fountain trickles into a beautiful pond covered with floating water lilies. You notice that stone benches and plinths are dotted around, many of them covered or surrounded by flowers and dusted with fallen petals. The green grass beneath you appears covered with confetti of white petals. Everywhere your gaze settles the many varieties of white flowers open in all their glory. You walk to the center of the stone temple and sit on a long bench. Around you the flowers whisper as the gentle breeze kisses them in greeting. Here, there is utter serenity. Total peace. You notice that the sky above you no longer shows a bright morning; instead you can see the swirl of planets sparkling in the night sky. Never before have you seen the stars so clearly, hundreds of thousands of individual lights dancing together in a universal song. This place is your connection to spirit, to the all that was, to the all that is, to the all that will be. This is your chakra temple.

(Long pause)

When you are ready, you can leave this place the way you came. Give blessings to each archway as you pass, and the flowers will return to their sleeping buds. As you leave the temple area, the white flowers close behind you... 10... The arch of purple beauty slowly closes as you pass... 9... The tiny blue flowers are already snapping shut one after the other as you walk beneath them... 8... The delicate green flowers have curled their petals inwards and shiver as you pass by... 7... The cascade of yellow flowers pull back into tight little buds as you walk under the arch... 6... The scent of orange blossom fades as the orange flowers close behind you... 5... Ahead are the deep red roses already closing their petals as you approach... 4... Leaving the maze you find yourself once more on the manicured lawn... 3... Walk away from the maze, up a gentle grassy incline... 2... You are returning to conscious awareness... 1... You return to your body, to the here and now. Become aware of your physical body. Release any tension your muscles hold, wiggle your toes, clench and relax your hands, roll your shoulders, turn your head from side to side. You are grounded in the here and now. You are relaxed, calm and re-energized. When you are ready, open your eyes.

Your energy levels will be high after this meditation, although your body will feel relaxed, so ground any excess energy before moving on through your day. It is always advisable to eat and drink after a meditation to bring yourself back to full awareness. This simple meditation is a wonderful way to open and balance your chakras, and can be done as a regular part of your spiritual practice.

Challenge and Opportunity Meditation

Close your eyes. Breathe deeply. You are about to journey into the deepest parts of self and reveal your greatest challenge and the keys of opportunity. The answers lie deep within you, deep inside your subconscious. As you breathe, fall deeper into yourself. Listen to your heartbeat, to the rushing of blood within your ears. Feel the pulsing of your blood, the waters of your body. Fall deeper still into the deep red black of your blood. Move with it, like the tides of your body, back and forth, ebb and flow. Be cocooned inside yourself as you were once cocooned in the womb. Here you are safe and warm, surrounded by the flesh of your being. Breathe deeply.

(Pause)

Become aware of the sense of space around you. You are no longer curled within your body, but standing still on damp grass. As the light cool breeze of early night awakens you, open your eyes and see the meadow around you. The hills roll across the countryside in every direction, illuminated by the starry sky and waxing moon. Ahead of you lies a barrow mound, as ancient as the landscape around you. You feel pulled towards the mound, and you know this is where you need to go. You walk ahead through long meadow grass, wildflowers, tall grass, brushing your legs as you walk. Creatures of the night rustle in the meadow around you, snuffling and rooting. Holding your arms out to your sides you let the long grass tickle your palms as you walk, the grasses rough and sticky, the sleepy wildflowers smooth and cool to the touch.

(Pause)

As you move closer to the barrow mound you can see the entrance is framed by three large stones covered with worn engravings, and the tunnel beyond drops deep into the earth. Standing at the entrance you can feel the deep chill of earth rising to greet you, the smell of peat and moss heavy in your nostrils. The stones are smooth to the touch, all roughness worn away by the passage of time and the kiss of the elements. As you step into the tunnel you can see the way ahead is full of dancing light and flickering shadows. The rough stone walls house flaming torches that leave pools of shifting darkness between them. On the path at your feet lies a short sword, its blade scarred and worn with use. As you lift the sword in your hand, you discover that it feels natural to you, like an extension of yourself. This sword has journeyed with you before, and vanquished many of your previous fears.

(Pause)

Carrying the sword before you, you head deeper into the mound, down into the earth, all around you stone and dirt, light and shadow. The ground is worn but uneven under your feet, rising and falling. The walls seem to move closer in places, the tunnel narrowing and bringing you closer to the heat of the burning torches. Down you walk, the passage twisting and turning, but always moving down, deep into the belly of Mother Earth.

(Pause)

The sloping path beneath your feet starts to level out and before you the tunnel suddenly widens into a dark cavern. It is here that you will discover your challenge. You know this place, for you have been here many times before. Remain at the edge of the tunnel, the cavern ahead of you. The light from the burning torches does not reach into the depths of the cavern, and the soft crackle of flame seems to echo through the space ahead. Stand strong and tall, be aware of the strength of your muscles. Feel the blood pumping through your heart and rushing in your ears. Listen to the sound of your breathing and concentrate on deep calm breaths. Breathe in. Breathe out. Be prepared to face whatever comes your way.

(Pause)

When you are ready, hold your sword before you and step into the cavern. As you step across the threshold you feel a pressure, as if you are pushing against an invisible barrier. The barrier gives way suddenly, pitching you into the darkness of the cavern. As soon as you step forward into the darkness you can hear rapid movement heading towards you. The ground shakes under your feet, and small rocks scatter and crash around you. Musty, long-trapped air rushes around you, warm and dry and dusty. The scent of burning fills your nose and blurs your vision. Out of the darkness something moves towards you and you raise your sword high in anticipation. You will defeat this challenge. This is your destiny.

(Pause)

Almost blind in the darkness, deafened by the crashing of rocks around you, thrown off balance by the ground shaking beneath your feet, you rely on instinct to defeat this challenge. Suddenly the sense of motion is no longer moving towards you, but almost upon you. With one fell motion you bring down your sword the instant you can see the being before you. With a scream, your challenge falls to the floor and lies still. You have won. Your challenge has been defeated. Gradually the light shifts and the cavern brightens. Now you can see the being that you have slain. Consider the form your challenge has chosen to take, and understand the message it brings you.

(Long pause)

When you feel ready to release the challenge, lay your sword upon the floor beside you. The form slowly fades into the atmosphere, leaving nothing but a locked wooden box behind. As you lift the box, you feel the weight of the box seems far greater than its size would determine. The box has strong iron bands around it, and a small black padlock linking them together. Breathe deeply and exhale slowly onto the lock. The lock opens with a sharp crack, and the lid of the box lies ajar. This box holds the symbol of your opportunity within it. As you raise the lid you will see an item that you can take with you. Concentrate upon this symbol and what it means to you. Hold it in your hands, turn it over, look at it from all angles and understand the deep significance it has in your life.

(Long pause)

When you are ready, collect your belongings and turn back towards the tunnel. As you cross the threshold, the cavern plunges into darkness behind you... 10... The walk back up the tunnel makes you feel lighter and less burdened... 9... As you walk, the burning torches behind you splutter out leaving the tunnel in darkness... 8... Keep walking up, each step bringing you closer to conscious awareness... 7... Soon you can see the entrance ahead of you, the starry night shining through... 6... As you reach the entrance, place your sword and the lock box on the path. Take the symbol of opportunity with you... 5... Leave the barrow mound and stand in the cool dark air... 4... The night breeze thrills your skin and makes you feel refreshed and alive... 3... Walk into the meadow, barrow mound behind you, the long grass brushing your legs as you pass... 2... Slowly the world around you starts to fade into shades of grey... 1... You are returning to conscious awareness. You return to your body, to the here and now. Become aware of your physical body. Release any tension your muscles hold, wiggle your toes, clench and relax your hands, roll your shoulders, turn your head from side to side. You are grounded in the here and now. You are relaxed, calm and re-energized. When you are ready, open your eyes.

This meditation can be very enlightening when we are facing a crossroads in our life, but it is not one I recommend on a regular basis. This is deep subconscious trancework, and is not to be taken lightly. If possible, have a trusted friend stay with you during this meditation, or better yet have them guide you during the meditation. Some of the forms that the challenge may take can be very distressing; on more than one occasion I have slain myself. Having a trusted friend or a skilled practitioner to support you as you process the experience is very beneficial. The symbol of opportunity may not be understood straight away, and that is to be expected. Very little that our subconscious tells us is without many layers of meaning. Use the symbol you are given as a contemplation and meditation exercise until you feel that you have learned all you can from it.

Divination

Many different practices and techniques are listed as divination, although the most commonly known and practiced technique with Paganism is the art of Tarot. Divination is a form of deep intuition, using a variety of tools and techniques, listening intently to all the overlapping and interconnected influences of a situation and interpreting the most likely outcome.

Sometimes, the very act of tuning in on this deep level and understanding the influences that have created the current situation can actually manifest a change in path or destiny. Sometimes, no matter how many times a person uses divination, the same issues will arise again and again. In this case they have not yet managed to resolve an issue, or continue to repeat past actions and choices that will affect their future in similar ways. There are cases where in order to progress spiritually we must face particular challenges, but even if the challenge itself is perceived as destiny, the path towards and beyond that challenge can vary greatly.

Whatever form of divination we use, it offers an insight to the current situation and the most likely future based upon that situation as well as the energetic response of the people involved. A conscious understanding of the information revealed within a divination reading can dramatically impact the possible future that the reading suggests. Divination is an act of guidance, an insight into past, current and future situations. Divination is possibility, probability, but not inevitability.

The art of divination requires a certain mindset, an ability to connect with the threads of possibility and fate as well as reading the current energetic status of a person or situation. The simple idea is to find a way of stepping outside of the day-to-day existence, and connecting with the energetic undercurrent influencing everything. Some practitioners feel the need to work their divination within a circle, but many practitioners simply attempt to "tune in" prior to starting by using breathwork, grounding and centering, or reciting a chant or prayer.

Use the following poetry and prose to inspire your mindset when preparing for any form of divination. You can tie these pieces into a ritual circle, or use them as meditations or chants prior to focusing upon your skills.

Guardian Evocation

My friends of deepest darkest night
Of shadow and mist and moonlight
Those often felt but seldom seen
I call to thee, I welcome thee
Part the veil, so that I may see
Part the veil, show truths to me
Part the veil, show what lies behind
In deepest parts of soul and mind
As I craft, I seek to reveal
The secrets hidden by the mystical veil

Goddess Guidance Request

Blessed Goddess,
Guide my hands to choose wisely
Guide my eyes so that I may see clearly
Guide my mind so that I may understand the messages
    received
Protect me as I work within this circle of prophecy
Let naught but love and highest good influence my craft
Blessed Be

This Light

I sit within the spotlight
The stage in darkness lies
Preparing to perform

The arts of times gone by
The light washes down
Upon my upturned face
My tools about me shine
Blessed by unearthly grace
Within the shadows I hear
Soft anticipating sighs
Waiting for my hands to move
And open up the eyes
And I feel blessed
Refreshed
And inspired to be
I craft
And bend
And prophesy
I spin
And weave
All manner of life
I bend
And blend
The Craft of the Wise
For this light is the perfect time
The blending of body and mind
A chance for us all to divine

Scrying

Look into the blackened glass
See the images of time gone past
Watch the sorrow, feel the pain
Hear the laughter amidst the rain
From this past we must learn
For it relives now as the wheel turns
What was once will be again
Time gone the time has come

We must accept all our fears
What was done will not be undone
Our future is held loosely
By the hands of our young
They cannot see beyond our words
Tales of life woven and spun
I can see images of the future
Within the darkness before me
But they appear older than the lives
Of those that spawned me
What have we done?
What will we do?
The images fade without answers
It is up to me and you.

Destiny

The cards slip through my hands
I drift into the world of unreality
Of possibilities
Probabilities
But never inevitabilities

Scry the Becoming

The reflection of the Divine
I look into your eyes
And see all that does not exist
I look into the Divine
Into the knowing eyes
And see that I do not exist, do not resist, do not become
I am you
You are me
I am one within all
All within one
I am the spiral of order

In the Divine chaos
I am the chaos
Unraveled
Undone
The reflection infinite
Contained and formed
By the boundary of understanding
The reflection of the Divine
I look into your eyes
And see all that has or will exist
I exist, I resist, I am becoming
I am you
You are me
I am made whole once more
As one within the All
Slowly I become
The reflection in blackened glass
Looking out at the Divine
Looking in at me

Focus Chant

Calm and breathe
Clear the mind
Seek the answers
And one will find

Blessed Fates

Blessed Fates
Speak to me
Tell me now
What will be
Speak of truths
From times gone by
That shape the way

That the future lies

Challenges and Opportunities

Whispered wisdom come to me
From divination and prophecy
Tales of the challenges yet to come
Choices made that cannot be undone
Ways that change may come to be
Futures filled with possibility

Tarot Chant

Choose a card
Read the past
See how choices
Come to last
Choose a card
Read a fate
See how life
Interrelates
Choose a card
Read the possibilities
See how life
Is filled with opportunity
Choose a card
Read and know
The past, the present
And where the path goes

Connection Chant

I am essence of all that is
All that was
All that will be
At my hands my eyes will see
All that is

Was and may be

Quick Blessing

Blessed tools
Speak to me
Of possibilities
Probabilities
And all that may yet be
So mote it be

Farewells and Blessings

A part of closing a ritual is to say thank you and farewell to all the participants of the ritual, both seen and unseen. Many farewells in formal ritual mimic the pattern of speech used in the opening portion of the ritual. Quite frankly this ritual component is a matter of politeness, rather than an energetic necessity, and I have attended many rituals where this part of the ritual is overlooked.

Of course, like any other use of language it does contain an energetic influence, primarily that of gratitude. Gratitude is an important mindset to cultivate, as it is key to our emotional well-being and happiness. It also cultivates a mentality of mutual respect and honor for all those who participate in our lives – not just in our acts of magic. A simple thing like saying farewell can carry an energetic influence that reaches far beyond ritual and into our day to day lives.

Bidding Farewell to the Goddess
Beloved Lady; Mother, Wisewoman and Daughter,
We thank you for your presence in this rite,
May you always reside in our hearts and minds,
As we bid you farewell this night
We extinguish this flame knowing it is but a symbol of you
Hail and farewell

Blessed be the gracious Goddess
Mother of all to whom we shall return
We thank you for blessing our gathering with your presence
In gratitude we say hail and farewell

Blessed Goddess
We thank you for your presence this night

Go if you must, stay if you will
With gratitude we say hail and farewell

Bidding Farewell to the God

Beloved Lord; Father, Sage and Son,
We thank you for your presence in this rite,
May you always reside in our hearts and minds,
As we bid you farewell this night
We extinguish this flame knowing it is but a symbol of you
Hail and farewell

Blessed be the Green God
Father of all to whom we shall return
We thank you for blessing our gathering with your presence
In gratitude we say hail and farewell

Blessed God
We thank you for your presence this night
Go if you must, stay if you will
With gratitude we say hail and farewell

Bidding Farewell to the Quarters

Farewell to the Quarters

Powers of North and Earth
Of fertile field and woodland shrine
We thank you for your presence here
In this blessed rite
Go if you wish, stay if you will
Hail and farewell

Powers of East and Air
Of wild storms and winds benign
We thank you for your presence here

In this blessed rite
Go if you wish, stay if you will
Hail and farewell

Powers of South and Fire
Of burning flame that lights the night
We thank you for your presence here
In this blessed rite
Go if you wish, stay if you will
Hail and farewell

Powers of West and Water
Of oceans deep and tears of mine
We thank you for your presence here
In this blessed rite
Go if you wish, stay if you will
Hail and farewell

Quarter Blessings

Blessings to West and Water
By peace of dusk I bid thee farewell
Go if you must
Stay if you will
Hail and farewell

Blessings to South and Fire
By heat of day I bid thee farewell
Go if you must
Stay if you will
Hail and farewell

Blessings to East and Air
By break of dawn I bid thee farewell
Go if you must

Stay if you will
Hail and farewell

Blessings to North and Earth
By dark of night I bid the farewell
Go if you must
Stay if you will
Hail and farewell

Brief Farewell to the Quarters

With earth we learned a new way
With the wind we sang in a new day
With the fire we burned to survive
With water we respected our lives
Hail and farewell to the elements of our world

Farewell Familial Quarters

Farewell blessings to West and Water
Sister of life and emotional tides
We thank your purity and understanding
In our circle of celebration
Go if you wish, stay if you will
Hail and farewell

Farewell blessings to South and Fire
Brother of destruction, creation and transformation
We thank your passion and vitality
In our circle of celebration
Go if you wish, stay if you will
Hail and farewell

Farewell blessings to East and Air
Father of word and whispered wisdom
We thank your thought and inspiration

In our circle of celebration
Go if you wish, stay if you will
Hail and farewell

Farewell blessings to North and Earth
Mother of all and womb of manifestation
We thank your strength and stability
In our circle of celebration
Go if you wish, stay if you will
Hail and farewell

Closing the Circle

Closing the circle is the practice of releasing the magic and energy used to create the boundary of the circle, and allowing it to return from whence it came. To some practitioners this is a case of grounding the energy into the earth, for others a case of releasing it into the atmosphere.

It is very common to use the athame to close the circle in the reverse method used to create the circle. The energy is drawn back into the blade and channeled through the practitioner into the earth. The black handle of the athame will retain a certain amount of the energy channeled and this energy can be accessed at a later date if needed. This is an energetic practice and requires no speech, but as with all aspects of ritual words are often spoken to define the intent – in this case the intent to release, to let go, and to leave the sacred space we created. For many practitioners the closing of the circle is also an opportunity to thank and farewell any participants, seen or unseen, and a spoken gratitude can easily be incorporated into a closing.

Formal Closing

Blessed circle cast around
I release thee unto the ground
Unto the air to scatter free
Unto the storms, unto the sea
Go find your home within the All
As circle is released, our boundary falls
So mote it be

Simple Closing

Blessed circle, purpose fulfilled
I release thee, by my Will

Closing and Farewell

Let us carry this magic in our hearts,
As our rite ends and we now depart
Bid fond farewell as the circle wanes
Merry met, merry part, merry we meet again

Simple Statement

Our circle open,
But never broken
Our rite is ended
So mote it be

Ground and Release

Where magic once abounded
Circle closed, energy grounded
Let it all go in peace and love
As below, 'tis so above

Keep to Silence

Keep to silence, hold your tongue
Our rite complete, our work is done
Go forth, be merry, leave this place
And bear the magic with all good grace

Extinguish the Flames

As we darken the flames of our bright circle
We know that their light still burns in the worlds beyond
May their spirit light our way in time of darkness
A ritual ended, but not forgotten
Merry met, merry part, merry we shall meet again

Release and Balance

Now our magic has been raised and released
We release the circle that contained it all

May the energy find its way to balance or purpose
And the site be at peace
Our rite has ended
So mote it be

Release from Purpose

I draw back the energy of the circle
And send it down to our Mother Earth
The circle is released from purpose to be reborn again
As I will it, so mote it be

Release from Bond

This circle has served well
Time has come to say farewell
I release the energy of its bond
And return it all to where it belongs
As above
So below

Merry Part and Merry Meet Again

Practice gratitude every day. Practice gratitude at every rite. Even if you work solitary as opposed to in a coven, grove or group, your rites are never just you. Remembering to thank and show gratitude for any spirit that joined you during your rite is a wonderful way of reaffirming the sacredness and interconnectedness of all things. If you do not include a separate farewell or incorporate a blessing of gratitude in your circle closing, then take a little opportunity after closing your circle to offer thanks or blessings to any participant, seen or unseen, and leave your ritual on a note of gratitude and joy.

Farewell Blessings
We bless all those who have attended
And participated in this rite
May you carry the joy from this celebration
In your hearts for many a night

Thanks to All
We thank all who attended the circle this night
All those seen and unseen who joined in this rite
Go if you must, stay if you will,
In fondness we say hail and farewell

Solitary Blessings
I am one within all,
And all within one
For support in the sacred
I offer my blessings and love

Bless Us All
Blessings to us all, each one of us a part of the Divine we

honored during this rite. May we carry the joy of this celebration in our hearts for many a night. Merry meet, merry part, and merry meet again.

Dedications and Initiations

If that which you seek, you find not within yourself, you will never find without.
– Doreen Valiente

The structure of this book hasn't allowed for an easy integration of dedication and initiation rituals, but no book based heavily upon Wiccan and degree-based Witchcraft training would be complete without a discussion of these important rites. Many paths of learning do not acknowledge a system of degrees or initiations, and many others perceive initiations to be purely spiritual rather than education-based affairs. Many new to the path of Witchcraft base the value of their training and learning upon these enigmatic initiation ceremonies, without a full understanding of what they actually mean.

A dedication is a formal ceremony that acknowledges a person's desire to dedicate themselves to a path of spiritual study and learning. It is a statement of commitment before the Gods, and a personal commitment to explore one's talents, develop skills, to attune with the natural energies of our universe, to honor the Divine within and without, and to work upon spiritual development. A dedication ceremony typically denotes a minimum of a year and a day to explore the path you have chosen, at which point you will have a better understanding of whether this path is the right one for you, or if you should seek an alternative form of training or study to continue your spiritual evolution.

A dedication ceremony may be solitary, or it may be presided over by a High Priest, High Priestess, or an entire coven or group. Even when officiated by another, a dedication is a private affair. Even if taken publically, a dedication is still a personal experience. No one can dedicate you but you. You must make the commitment to yourself and to your Gods.

An initiation is twofold. Within personal spirituality a Divine initiation is the turning point of spiritual awareness, a point in one's life where the integration of study and learning creates a shift in the way that one perceives and experiences the world around them. These initiations often come with a spiritual, emotional, or mental crisis, suddenly or gradually, as we face old dynamics and behavior patterns and challenge our previous perceptions.

They can be uncomfortable experiences for many, and extremely unpleasant for some, as we are shedding an old familiar skin and learning to step forward newly empowered. However, an initiation is not a negative experience; it is more akin to a breakthrough rather than a breakdown. It is a challenge of our newfound understanding, and a transitional period of personal growth. The process of initiation leaves us feeling stronger, more aware of ourselves and our capabilities, and with a better understanding of our personal spirituality.

The other form of initiation is that of an outer ceremonial acknowledgement of these inner transformations, often within your coven or group. It is usually taken at the completion of a period of study, often no less than a year and a day of training and on many occasions several years after the training begins. It is a ceremony that considers a level of spiritual development, successful integration of new skills, a development of talents and abilities, and a certain connection with the Divine. At this point many covens will reveal additional information or education, or allow for different roles and responsibilities within the group.

In some groups initiations are treated like educational degrees; when one reaches the end of a period of study an initiation is granted. Although on many occasions the time period of training does coincide with a personal, spiritual Divine initiation, this isn't always the case. In the cases where a student places the value of their training on the ceremonial initiation without experiencing the spiritual shift that also occurs, the student can experience some challenges and difficulties when the Divine initiation does eventually occur.

Of course in some situations the integration of learning never happens, and we encounter High Priests and Priestesses with their "Black Belt in Witchcraft" without the experience or education to support others or fulfil the role of ministry within a community. Conversely, I have also witnessed some wonderful, compassionate, highly educated and spiritual people who have never been acknowledged through a degree-based initiation system and experienced the prejudice of others who subsequently devalue their worth despite their obvious capabilities.

In the system of training I first experienced, an initiation within the group was not completed until the mentor, High Priest or High Priestess saw the spiritual shift associated with a Divine initiation. This shift may be very obvious, even to those not involved in the same path of learning, or it may be revealed through the relationships and communication of the student. At this point it is understood that the student and the Gods have reached a new level of understanding between themselves, and that the student has or is experiencing an integration of the spiritual philosophies and magical training.

I have experienced these Divine initiations and the challenges that often present themselves at the same time, and I have witnessed it over and over with others. Although the surrounding impact on one's life can occasionally be an upheaval of beliefs, values and understanding, I have always found Divine initiations to be wonderful, enlightening and empowering experiences. Honoring that transition within your group can also be a very affirming experience and it is a blessing to look back and see how far we have travelled on our journey of spiritual self-discovery.

In several systems of degree-based training I have heard the unfortunate phrase that when it comes to Witchcraft it "takes one to make one", and whilst I respect many of the practitioners who hold this view, I personally believe this concept integrates into a new student's psyche in a very unhealthy way. It instills the idea that one cannot be a Witch without another Witch at best acknowledging your spiritual experiences, and at worst bestowing the rights and powers of Witchcraft.

No one person has power over your power. Your inherent worth is not defined by the views of another. Knowledge, power and wisdom are not given upon a silver platter; they are earned through dedication, commitment, hard work and experience. Regardless of practice within a coven or solitary setting, a student can certainly do the work to develop their skills and magic.

A coven or group may bestow a new name or title during initiation, and it is quite common for solitaries to adopt a new craft name during dedication or initiation. However, do not expect someone to value your worth based on a title, whether it be self-imposed or bestowed by a group; you must learn to stand on your own merit. Be honest with yourself and take responsibility for your training; if you have not done the work, if you feel you have more to learn or you simply don't feel ready, then don't undergo your ceremonial initiation. If you consider yourself a Witch, solitary or otherwise, then do the work to embody that belief.

Many share my views on the process of initiation, but many do not. Some will openly argue against the descriptions I have laid out here, and each person is entitled to voice their truth as they see it. This is my truth, based on my experiences. Initiations are deeply personal, spiritual experiences between you and the Divine, and not simply a merit of time studied. I have no issues with how other training systems incorporate initiations into their structure, my only serious disagreement lies in the belief that one cannot become their authentic spiritual self without the acknowledgement of another who determines their spiritual worth. This belief is misguided at best and psychologically damaging at worst, and must be addressed for what it is and not simply perpetuated in the name of tradition.

Every person, every experience, shapes the person you become. Every choice, every action, every reaction, shapes the person you become.

Every teacher or mentor can guide your learning experiences, but only you can integrate that learning.

No one makes you a Witch, but you.

A witch is a witch is a witch is a witch. If someone is genuinely devoted to the ways of the Old Gods and the magic of nature, in my eyes they're valid, especially if they can use the old witch powers. In other words, it isn't what people know, it's what they are.
– Doreen Valiente

The Method of Dedication and Initiation

Every group or coven that uses a degree-based system of learning will have slightly different methods of dedication and initiation. They are formal ceremonies, and as such will usually involve a full circle casting: cleansing the space, purification of the participants, casting of the circle, evoking the elements, Elementals or Guardians, and calling the Gods.

At this point, the process varies dependant on your path. Some groups will expect an initiate to be skyclad, blindfolded and bound, others do not. Most groups will present some form of challenge, either by creating situations of fear and trust by exposing the initiate to the elements, by stopping the initiate outside the circle with an athame held to their chest and asking for perfect love and perfect trust, by scourging, or by verbally challenging the initiate's motives upon entering the circle. Some groups will use all of these techniques, or similar techniques. The initiates, after successfully facing their challenges, will often make a speech to verbalize their past experiences, their current motives, and their future intent. This is an opportunity to reflect upon the journey so far, and think about what they want to achieve from their continuing spiritual studies. At this point, the initiate is presented to the elements and the Gods for their blessings. Other ritual aspects, such as a cakes and ale rite or a symbolic Great Rite, may also be included. Once the ritual is complete, the circle is closed as usual and an informal celebration may continue.

Although the method of an initiation by its nature can be unsettling, it should never be a situation where initiates are forced to participate in activities without full knowledge and consent. An initiation is a form of challenge, not least because it asks us, "Is this really what we want for ourselves?" Even if the answer is yes, that does not mean that you must submit to activities you feel are wrong.

Any true spiritual introspection can raise issues and can be uncomfortable, and facing those issues or fears is an important part of spiritual development. Stepping outside our comfort zone can lead us into new areas of personal and spiritual enlightenment. If you are working within a coven or group, talk to the High Priest or Priestess about any concerns you may have about initiations. Discuss the methods used within the group, and actively participate in developing a ritual that works to the best advantage for your growth, a ritual that both challenges and empowers. If you cannot work with the group to develop a ritual, and you are not comfortable with the method of initiation the group provides, then consider continuing your training elsewhere or delay your initiation until you fully understand and feel prepared to complete the ritual.

Some covens insist on working skyclad, but if you are not comfortable or happy to be naked when working with others then that may not be the group for you – or it may provide an opportunity to develop body confidence.

Some groups may include an element of scourging in their

rites, but some individuals are not comfortable with this concept for many reasons, and personal experiences must be acknowledged. If a High Priest or Priestess insists on sexual intercourse as a method of initiation, then leave the group and find some support. Sexual activities can be a powerful form of magic, but it must be safe and consensual and not used as coercion, bribery or assault. If the High Priest or Priestess is not your current sexual partner, or if the entire group expects you to be sexually involved during the process, then I would feel safe to say that this is an unhealthy and possibly dangerous situation to be in.

If the person who officiates your rite is your current sexual partner, if you and any other participants are aware and comfortable with a sexual element to your rite, then it is not for me to say that such a thing is wrong – indeed it can be a very potent experience. My only concern is that every initiate feels safe and supported, not manipulated or abused.

Talk to other group members or close friends, meditate upon the situation, discuss it with your guides and your Gods. Make sure that the ceremonial initiation is something you want and feel ready to do, and that you feel safe and secure in the method of initiation. I cannot stress enough that an initiation may be challenging, but it needs to be challenging in a healthy manner. It will also be empowering and inspiring, and an affirmation of the magical journey you are experiencing.

For solitary practitioners, dedications and initiations are often overlooked as they tend to revolve around group and coven-based training systems. Despite that fact that ceremonial initiations are most often found in a degree-based training systems, a solitary practitioner may also create a personal, solitary ritual initiation if they wish to. Some will disagree with me on this matter, but I believe that a ceremonial initiation is a form of life rite and each person is entitled to mark life transitions in front of their Gods.

When working solitary one must be very aware of their

personal spiritual development. A ceremonial initiation cannot be based solely upon a degree-based education system, as there is no group, coven or leader to reinforce the learning, abilities and skills of the student. Instead the ceremonial initiation is based upon the Divine initiation – that point in your life when your spiritual studies and magical training create a shift within your physical, mental and emotional life. This can be hard to observe, especially if the shift comes gradually, but this transition is every magical practitioner's true initiation.

Completing a ceremonial initiation after this point is an outer acknowledgement of that inner shift. Solitary initiations do not come with degree level certificates or a particular title, because these things do not exist outside of particular groups or covens. Titles hold little meaning to those outside of that particular path of study, so please don't get attached to the idea that an initiation gives you power or presence. You need your own power and presence in order to experience the initiation.

A Solitary Initiation Rite

Prepare the space you wish to use by cleaning and tidying, and organizing your altar. Your sacred space will be as unique as you are, as will your altar. Many altars will include a representation of the elements and the Goddess and God; candles or crystals to mark the quarters; salt, chalice of water and athame. You will also need incense or white sage to smudge yourself, a mirror, a white candle, a pen and paper, and a cauldron or metal pot you can safely burn paper in.

Gather any tools you wish to bless and consecrate during the rite, and any offerings you wish to make to the Divine. Make sure everything you need is within easy reach.

If possible, take a hot bath infused with salt and sage prior to the ritual. Use one of the self purification rites during your bath or a simple chant, and meditate upon your journey to this point. Once cleansed and relaxed, enter your ritual space – naked, if you feel comfortable to be so.

Light your incense or sage and allow the smoke to envelop you.

> I am a child of this world
> With all that it means
> I am a child of spirit
> With all that it means
> I cleanse my body
> I cleanse my mind
> I cleanse my heart
> I cleanse my soul
> Each aspect refreshed and blessed
> In harmony, in rest
> I face the future with love and trust
> To do all I can, and all I must.

Use your hands to move the sacred smoke around your ritual space deosil (clockwise.)

> By my hand, by my will
> I clear this place of all its ills
> By my will, by my hand
> I make a sacred space of this land.

Take your athame and draw a circle around your sacred space, pulling the energy up from the earth, through you and directing out from your blade. Start in the North, your foundation element, and move deosil around your space, slightly overlapping your starting position. At the end of your casting, raise your blade above your head, pointing towards the sky, and then lower it to the earth to complete your circle.

> I draw this circle about me, in the presence of the elements and Divine spirit

That I may be aided by the Lord and Lady and be blessed by
my work this night
The boundary of my circle lies below my feet,
Above my head
Around my body
That I may work within a sphere of protection and love
And protection and love may work within me
As above, 'tis so below
The circle is charged and cast, so mote it be.

*Face North and using your athame draw an invoking pentagram with
your blade.*

Greetings and blessings to North and Earth,
By dark of night I welcome thee
In cycles of seasons forever changing
I accept your influence within and around me
I seek you out and call your name
To be with me on this sacred night
May your qualities be found within me
And your blessings be bestowed upon this rite.

*Face East and using your athame draw an invoking pentagram with
your blade.*

Greetings and blessings to East and Air,
By break of dawn I welcome thee
In breeze and storms and winds of change
I accept your influence within and around me
I seek you out and call your name
To be with me on this sacred night
May your qualities be found within me
And your blessings be bestowed upon this rite.

Face South and using your athame draw an invoking pentagram with your blade.

Greetings and blessings to South and Fire,
By heat of day I welcome thee
In forging fires of transformation
I accept your influence within and around me
I seek you out and call your name
To be with me on this sacred night
May your qualities be found within me
And your blessings be bestowed upon this rite.

Face West and using your athame draw an invoking pentagram with your blade.

Greetings and blessings to West and Water,
By peace of dusk I welcome thee
In ebb and flow and tides of change
I accept your influence within and around me
I seek you out and call your name
To be with me on this sacred night
May your qualities be found within me
And your blessings be bestowed upon this rite.

If you use a candle to represent the Goddess, light your candle now. If you have a statue of the Goddess on your altar, place your hand upon it. If you have neither, center yourself and raise your arms to draw the energy down into your sacred space. As you welcome the presence of the Goddess cross your arms over your chest.

Beloved Lady, my Feminine Divine
I invite you here at this time outside of time
To a place of trust and love between
All that is and is yet unseen

Pause a while with me during this rite
Bless me with your wisdom and watchful sight
Let your compassionate Divinity
Be present within and around me
Hail and Welcome!

Pause until you feel the presence of the Goddess with you, then re-enter yourself and prepare to evoke the God.

Beloved Lord, my Masculine Divine
I invite you here at this time outside of time
To a place of trust and love between
All that is and is yet unseen
Pause a while with me during this rite
Bless me with your wisdom and watchful sight
May the heat and the hunter now abound
Within me and all around
Hail and Welcome!

Pause until you feel the presence of the God join you. Take as much time as you need to adjust to the presence of the Divine.

Great God, Beloved Goddess
Tonight you grace me with your presence
You are the embodiment of the Divine
A Divinity that has touched my life
From my heart to yours
I offer you love and gratitude
Blessed be.

(Please consider writing your own prose to outline your thoughts, feelings and intent. This should come from the heart, and can be utterly spontaneous if you wish. The following text may inspire or focus what you wish to say.)

I call to you tonight to honor the presence of magic within my life and to acknowledge the transformation of my life. Over the last few years of study I have felt myself change, not into someone new, but into a truer version of myself. I have laughed and cried, loved, worked hard, and faced the fears that lie in the shadows of my soul. I have learned to see the Divine around me and within me, and honor that Divinity without and within. I have dropped many masks and stand naked in form and thought to claim my power and be true to my magical nature, as One within the All.

At this point you may wish to write down any issues, fears or challenges you are ready to let go of. These can be lit in the flame of your white candle, and left to burn in your cauldron.

Tonight I set free the things that hinder my growth. With forgiveness, understanding and new perspective I let go of all that no longer serves me, and prepare to face my future with the burning desire of transformation.

Raise the mirror and gaze into your own reflection, a reflection of the Divine. If you wish to, verbalize any hopes or intentions you have for your future studies. Meditate upon your reflection until you can see yourself with detachment, as the Divine with human face.

I am power, I am grace
I am spirit with human face
I see the Divine, the Divine sees me
I am within the Divine, the Divine within me

Sprinkle some salt into your chalice of water. Raise your athame above the chalice and slowly move the blade down into the water. This is the union of blade and chalice, of God and Goddess, and is an act of power and purification.

As the athame is to the masculine,
So the chalice is to the feminine
For what one lacks the other gives
There is no greater power than that of love
As above, so below
As within, so without
So mote it be.

Sprinkle some of the water upon yourself as a blessing from the Gods.

I call the blessings of the Goddess and God upon me!
Blessed be my feet that walk the path of the God and Goddess
Blessed be my sexuality that honors life
Blessed be my heart that holds love for my path
Blessed be my lips that speak the sacred names
Blessed be my mind that houses knowledge of the ways.

Take as long as you need in the sacred circle. Meditate, write, practice divination, talk to your Gods, chant, sing or dance. Take this opportunity to cleanse, consecrate and bless any ritual tools. You can sprinkle the consecrated salt water on your tools, with a simple blessing of "May it serve me well and harm me none". When you are ready, say farewell to the Gods and elements and close the circle.

Beloved Lady, Beloved Lord
I thank you for your presence this night
And for your guidance in my sacred rite
Go if you wish
Stay if you will
In love I bid thee hail and farewell.

Face West and draw a banishing pentagram with your athame.

Blessings to West and Water

By peace of dusk I bid thee farewell
Go if you wish
Stay if you will
Hail and farewell.

Face South and draw a banishing pentagram with your athame.

Blessings to South and Fire
By heat of day I bid thee farewell
Go if you wish
Stay if you will
Hail and farewell.

Face East and draw a banishing pentagram with your athame.

Blessings to East and Air
By break of dawn I bid thee farewell
Go if you wish
Stay if you will
Hail and farewell.

Face North and draw a banishing pentagram with your athame.

Blessings to North and Earth
By dark of night I bid thee farewell
Go if you wish
Stay if you will
Hail and farewell.

Starting in the North and moving widdershins (anti-clockwise) around the circle, draw back the energy you used to create your sacred space. The energy will move through the blade, through you, and back into the earth. Overlap your starting position slightly and conclude by raising your athame to the sky and then lower it to the earth.

I draw back the energy of the circle
And send it down to our Mother Earth
The circle is released from purpose to be reborn again
As I will it, so mote it be.
I am one within all,
And all within one
For support in the sacred
I offer my blessings and love
My rite is ended
So mote it be

Sample Rituals

The following chapter contains a variety of sample rituals using the component format displayed within this book. I have not included a step-by-step guide for participants, or information on correspondences, purely sample scripts and suggestions. This book does make the assumption that the reader has a basic understanding of ritual, either from a folk perspective or from more formal training. In order to create the most effective ritual possible, you will need to consider the energetic influences of more than just ritual language, by considering phases of the moon and sun; cycle of the seasons; time of day or night; natural biorhythms; impact of color, scent, sound; and any tools, techniques and practices you wish to include.

Ritual is much more than a script, it is a sacred act of being present and participating in our spirituality. It is experiential, it is inspired, it is encompassing, it is the limitless contained within a boundary. Sacred script, sacred sound, is an important part of ritual as an act of magic itself, but try not to get lost in the process of creating a ritual. If you are to lose and find yourself, then lose yourself to the energetic effect of your ritual. Lose yourself in the magic and find yourself in the wonder of creation in action.

Each ritual included here is designed around the aspect of Feminine and Masculine Divinity, not specific deities. If you wish to work with a particular God or Goddess, the invocation/evocation sections of the rituals can be easily adapted by replacing the more generic terminology with a detailed invocation related to your chosen deity. Once evoked, a devotional may also be added to welcome and honor your deity.

I have limited the number of participants present within these sample rituals for ease, but I would suggest that rituals be tailored to the number of participants. If you are working solitary, you may wish to simplify these rituals further or you may be comfortable using all the aspects by yourself. If you have more participants, you may wish to involve each member by delegating portions of the spoken ritual, or by clearly defining physical roles and actions. If you are operating a very large ritual or open circle you may have to adapt these rituals to cope with such large numbers of non-speaking participants, by creating a more theatrical setting that captures each participant's imagination or by involving more chanting or dancing that enables everyone present to participate on a more active level.

Dependent on the path you walk you may believe that some of the components of these rituals are unnecessary, or that I have neglected to include practices and techniques considered essential to your way of working.

I certainly do not believe that the ritual format presented within this book is the only true or right way of practicing, and indeed many of my own personal rituals vary in style and form. Be clear and honest with yourself as to what you deem important and necessary when creating your own ritual, and work towards designing a ritual with maximum energetic impact. This book is a framework and foundation to build upon, to inspire those who wish to create bespoke rituals or blessings, and to encourage every magical practitioner to consider the impact and power of their words.

I offer these samples as an option to use or adapt to suit your purpose, and hopefully to inspire your own unique rituals.

Please note the short hand:

HPS: High Priestess
HP: High Priest
HP/S: High Priest or High Priestess
NQ: Participant representing the North / Earth Quarter
EQ: Participant representing the East / Air Quarter
SQ: Participant representing the South / Fire Quarter
WQ: Participant representing the West / Water Quarter

Baby Blessing

A Baby Blessing, sometimes called a Wiccaning, is a celebration of new life, an opportunity for friends and family to gather and welcome the new child's presence, an opportunity to introduce the child to your Gods and guides, and a ceremony to acknowledge the role of any legal guardians, godparents, or spiritual supporters for the child's upbringing.

On some occasions the Baby Blessing is also used as a naming ceremony, and the child's name is not revealed to friends and family until this point. For families with mixed spiritual beliefs, a Baby Blessing may incorporate more traditional aspects or language associated with their path, or even follow a more familiar format such as a modern Christening rite. There is no set time to hold a Baby Blessing, although they are most common within the first year of the child's life.

The following ritual is just one example of a Baby Blessing, but this ceremony can easily be tailored to the needs and wishes of each family.

HPS: I cleanse this space of all negativity,
Let only love remain within
This is a sacred place for all to be.
Cleansed and consecrated for rite to begin.
NQ: I call upon the element of Earth to be with us during this rite of celebration
Bring forth your qualities of security and stability, and lend us your wisdom
Hail and welcome!
All: Hail and welcome!
EQ: I call upon the element of Air to be with us during this rite of celebration
Bring forth your qualities of inspiration and intellect, and lend

us your wisdom
Hail and welcome!
All: Hail and welcome!
SQ: I call upon the element of Fire to be with us during this rite of celebration
Bring forth your qualities of passion and vitality, and lend us your wisdom
Hail and welcome!
All: Hail and welcome!
WQ: I call upon the element of Water to be with us during this rite of celebration
Bring forth your qualities of compassion and understanding, and lend us your wisdom
Hail and welcome!
All: Hail and welcome!
HPS: I cast about this place
A circle of love and devotion
A circle to protect the new life we honor today
A circle to contain the love of kith and kin, to bathe the child in love's blessings
From Mother Earth below us, to Father Sky above us, may this circle be cast
So Mote It Be!
All: So Mote It Be!
HPS: I call upon the gracious Lady, Feminine Divine, Mother of all
Hear us now, your children
We ask you to grace us with your presence as we honor a new life
Be with us as we celebrate in love and joy
Share your qualities as a Divine Mother and bless this new child of the world
Hail and welcome!
All: Hail and welcome!

HPS: I call upon the wise Lord, Masculine Divine, Father of all
Hear us now, your children
We ask you to grace us with your presence as we honor a new life
Be with us as we celebrate in love and joy
Share your qualities as a Divine Father and bless this new child of the world
Hail and welcome!
All: Hail and welcome!
HPS: We gather here today to honor the new life before us, to marvel in the wonders that love creates, and to share in the first steps of this child's journey. Before us is a being of pure potential, a little person with big dreams yet to manifest. Let us all be reminded of the excitement of discovering the world around us, the wonder of simple things, and the joy of a loving family around us. Each person here today brings the gift of love and laughter into this child's life, but several people stand apart from the crowd as playing distinct roles in this child's life.
HPS: May the parents step forward. From your love you are presenting a new life into this world, and from your dedication and commitment you will support and encourage your little loved one as they learn and grow. What name do you bless this child with?

Parents to state child's full name, and meaning of the name, qualities of the name or reasons for choosing the name if they wish.

HPS to the child: This name is yours child. It holds the qualities your parents dream for you, but it is as unique as your own essence. Make this name yours, let it be a true reflection of who you are and who you wish to be.
HPS to the parents: What promises do you make to your child this day?

Parents' individual statements. These may be written in advance, or simply spoken from the heart on the day.

Example Statement: We promise to love you, and more, we promise to remind you that we love you in word and action. We promise to guide you, and more, we promise to lead by example. We promise to support you, and more, we promise to display that support by supporting others around us. We promise to honor you for who you are not who we wish you to be, and more, we promise to be a reflection of that by living honestly and authentically ourselves.

HPS: This child is blessed by the support of their parents and their family, and also by the support of chosen guardians and guides. Would the chosen guardians of this child step forward and share your unique gifts?

1st: I offer you security and comfort throughout your life, and I promise to share in the wonder of the world and its seasons around you.

2nd: I offer you inspiration and knowledge, and I promise to share in the wonder of language, song and the written word.

3rd: I offer you support and enthusiasm, and I promise to share in your excitement of discovery, learning and active play.

4th: I offer you empathy and understanding, and I promise to share my experiences as you navigate the complexities of human interaction and relationships.

5th: I offer you peace and serenity, and I promise to share wisdom of the many spiritual beliefs of our world and encourage you to find your own sense of spirituality.

HPS: Today you have been given wonderful gifts child, may they bless you again and again in the years to come. May the Lord and Lady hold you close to their hearts and watch over you as you grow. May the elements be kind to you as you learn to find your way in the world. May you be blessed by your ancestors and loved by your peers. Today, and each day forth, may you be safe in the knowledge that you are loved.

Pause.

On this day we stand together in a circle of family and friends, kith and kin, to greet this child (say child's name here) into the world. I ask you now, who will love and cherish this child?
All: We will!
HPS: Who will support and encourage this child?
All: We will!
HPS: Who walk with this child as they journey through life?
All: We will!
HPS: Welcome to the world little one
Still holding fast to memories of heart beat and blood rush
From the living waters of your mother's womb
You now face the bright world around you
We marvel in your presence
Most cherished soul
Be safe and comforted in our arms
As we hold you in our hearts
Be at peace
Be calm
You are safe
You are loved
You are welcomed home
Welcome (child's name)!
All: Welcome (child's name)!
HPS: Now in love, in joy, in celebration, let us say farewell to the elements, close our circle, then eat, drink and be merry!
HPS: I thank and bless the Lord and Lady for their presence here on this joyous day. Go if you must, but stay if you will. Blessed be!
All: Blessed be!

WQ: I thank and bless the element of Water for their presence here on this joyous day. Go if you must, but stay if you will. Blessed be!

All: Blessed be!

SQ: I thank and bless the element of Fire for their presence here on this joyous day. Go if you must, but stay if you will. Blessed be!

All: Blessed be!

EQ: I thank and bless the element of Air for their presence here on this joyous day. Go if you must, but stay if you will. Blessed be!

All: Blessed be!

NQ: I thank and bless the element of Earth for their presence here on this joyous day. Go if you must, but stay if you will. Blessed be!

All: Blessed be!

HPS: Circle of love and devotion,

Your task is complete and we graciously return your energy to our Mother the Earth.

This circle is open, yet never broken.

So mote it be!

All: So mote it be!

Rite of Passage – Child to Maiden

It is typical that a ritual to honor an emerging womanhood is completed by women loved dearly by the maiden being honored. Mothers, grandmothers, aunts, sisters, female relatives and friends should all be in attendance. It is more unusual to have men at this rite, purely as it is a ritual designed around female menstruation, but I for one see no issues in men attending should the maiden wish to be surrounded by their love and focus. Female energy and power is important to a rite like this, but a child becoming woman is not solely a celebration for other women. Men can and should celebrate the young woman in their midst, providing that all circle members feel comfortable with the addition of masculine energy.

I have seen rituals designed around both male and female participants, purely female participants, and rituals led by women prior to a more public celebration involving both men and women. Only you can know what will be most appropriate for the maiden you are honoring, and since it is a day of celebration for her it is best to design a ritual she will be most comfortable participating in. It is also quite traditional to allow the maiden a more active role within this ceremony, the level of which is determined by the High Priestess. I have included the maiden's role as cleansing and consecrating the circle in this example.

Some paths also include active components to the ritual, such as the maiden crawling between the legs of the other female circle members (symbolizing a rebirth) or being lifted by other members before being placed back on her feet (symbolizing the letting go from her mother and her first steps as a woman), but I have often found that these active components cause embarrassment and are not conducive to the maiden's ritual process. In my experience, story sharing and gift giving create a more open and relaxed atmosphere for the maiden, but again this is for you to decide what works best for your circle. Below is an example ritual that you may use or adapt as you see fit.

Maiden: Sweep and cleanse!
Sweep and clear!
Chase away all doubt and fear
Sweep the circle!
Sweep this place!
Soon to be a sacred space.
HPS: I charge and bless this salt and water
Sacred to our Divine Mother
With scattering around this place
I consecrate this sacred space
Blessed be.
All: Blessed be.
HPS: By the earthly body of my flesh,
The air of my breath,
The fire of my spirit,
The living waters of my womb,
I cast this circle in honor of the Goddess that birthed us all,
And the Goddess within me
Be now a place of power and peace
Consecrated and sacred to all within
As I will it, so shall it be.
All: So mote it be!
NQ: Greetings and blessings to North and Earth,
By dark of night I welcome thee
In cycles of seasons forever changing
I accept your influence within and around me
I seek you out and call your name
To be with me on this sacred night
May your qualities be found within me
And your blessings be bestowed upon this rite.
All: Hail and welcome!

EQ: Greetings and blessings to East and Air,
By break of dawn I welcome thee
In breeze and storms and winds of change
I accept your influence within and around me
I seek you out and call your name
To be with me on this sacred night
May your qualities be found within me
And your blessings be bestowed upon this rite.
All: Hail and welcome!
SQ: Greetings and blessings to South and Fire,
By heat of day I welcome thee
In forging fires of transformation
I accept your influence within and around me
I seek you out and call your name
To be with me on this sacred night
May your qualities be found within me
And your blessings be bestowed upon this rite.
All: Hail and welcome!
WQ: Greetings and blessings to West and Water,
By peace of dusk I welcome thee
In ebb and flow and tides of change
I accept your influence within and around me
I seek you out and call your name
To be with me on this sacred night
May your qualities be found within me
And your blessings be bestowed upon this rite.
All: Hail and welcome!
HPS: Beloved Lady, our Feminine Divine
We ask you here at this time outside of time
To a place of trust and love between
All that is and is yet unseen
Pause a while with us during this rite
Bless us with your wisdom and watchful sight
Let your compassion, experience and grace

Work through this Priestess in your place
Hail and welcome!

All: Hail and welcome!

HPS: Beloved Lord, our Masculine Divine
We ask you here at this time outside of time
To a place of trust and love between
All that is and is yet unseen
Pause a while with us during this rite
Bless us with your wisdom and watchful sight
May the heat and the hunter now coarse through
This humble Priestess that speaks for you
Hail and welcome!

All: Hail and welcome!

HPS: We gather here today, a sacred circle of women,
To celebrate the emerging woman in our midst
We are proud to be a part of this maiden's journey as she steps towards womanhood
And we recall our own journey, so similar and yet each one unique
We offer our experiences and any words of wisdom
In this circle of sharing.

Each person should offer a story, some advice or wisdom – practical or spiritual – that may assist the young lady as she heads towards womanhood.

HPS: Like the cycles of the beloved moon, you wax and wane
From the blessings of your mother's womb, to the blessings of your own womb
The time has come to celebrate your changing body
And the mind that changes with new awareness and responsibility
As young as you are now, this stage is your first step into the world of Woman

Into the world of the sacred feminine
Your body will take on new cycles now,
New rhythms,
New tides of ebb and flow, wax and wane
As a maiden flourishing, you will need to adjust to the cycle
of your body
And the effects it will have upon the waters of your emotions
This is a time of change
But all things change
It is the way of the world, and the way of woman
As a woman soon to be, we honor you as maidens we once
were
With love and pride
We see you travel along your journey
From child, to maiden, to woman
Blessed be your journey.
All: Blessed be!
HPS: From the sun to the corn
From the corn to the flour
From the flour to the bread
May we be blessed by this bounty
May we never hunger
We consecrate this bread in the name of the Masculine Divine
Eat and be merry.

*At this point the bread is passed around the circle, a piece broken off for
each member. As the bread is passed from hand to hand, the blessing of
"Eat and be merry" should be spoken by the giver to the receiver.*

HPS: From the rain to the vine
From the vine to the fruit
From the fruit to the wine
May we be blessed by this bounty
May we never thirst

We consecrate this wine in the name of the Feminine Divine
Drink and be merry.

*At this point the wine goblet is passed around the circle, each member
taking a drink. As the wine goblet is passed from hand to hand, the
blessing of "Drink and be merry" should be spoken by the giver to the
receiver.*

HPS: At this time it is appropriate to simply enjoy each
other's company, and to honor our maiden of the moon with
any gifts you may wish to share. Please eat, drink, be
comfortable and celebrate this time of change with the famil-
iarity of family and friendship.

*Spend some time just enjoying each other's company, sharing stories,
telling jokes or giving gifts. This is a time to help your maiden feel
comfortable about the changes she is facing, and a safe friendly atmos-
phere may also assist her in raising any questions, concerns or fears she
may have about the changes to her body, her emotions or her day-to-day
life. Dealing with any issues that may surface is the concern of the
High Priestess, please be observant and direct the appropriate people to
discuss the issues with honesty and integrity.*

HPS: Beloved Lady; Mother, Wisewoman and Daughter,
We thank you for your presence in this rite,
May you always reside in our hearts and minds,
As we bid you farewell this night
Hail and farewell!
All: Hail and farewell!
HPS: Beloved Lord; Father, Sage and Son,
We thank you for your presence in this rite,
May you always reside in our hearts and minds,
As we bid you farewell this night
Hail and farewell!

All: Hail and farewell!

WQ: Blessings to West and Water

By peace of dusk I bid thee farewell

Go if you must

Stay if you will

Hail and farewell

All: Hail and farewell!

SQ: Blessings to South and Fire

By heat of day I bid thee farewell

Go if you must

Stay if you will

Hail and farewell

All: Hail and farewell!

EQ: Blessings to East and Air

By break of dawn I bid thee farewell

Go if you must

Stay if you will

Hail and farewell

All: Hail and farewell!

NQ: Blessings to North and Earth

By dark of night I bid thee farewell

Go if you must

Stay if you will

Hail and farewell

All: Hail and farewell!

HPS: Our circle open,

But never broken

Our rite is ended

So mote it be.

All: So mote it be!

HPS: Blessings to all those who have attended and participated in this rite. May you carry the joy from this celebration

In your hearts for many a night.

Rite of Passage – Child to Lord / Squire

A rite of passage for a child moving to manhood is often presided over and attended by male participants – father, grand-fathers, uncles, brothers, male family and friends. However, in the spirit of equality and celebration, I honestly see no reason why women should be excluded from this celebration providing that the young lord in question is happy to have the feminine influence within the ritual. For the mother of the young lord, this will be an emotional time and participating in the ritual may actually assist the mother in the process of accepting her child's progression to adulthood.

It is ultimately the decision of the young lord as to who participates in the rite, as it is a day of celebration tailored around him. If the young lord feels more comfortable with a purely male influence, especially if he intends to raise questions or concerns about his changing needs, then that should be honored and respected. I have seen rites of passage that involved many men and women from the community in a wonderful, joyous celebration, and a more private intimate gathering held afterwards with just a few men. There are many ways that ritual and celebration can be adapted to suit the personal needs of the participants. Below is an example ritual that may be used or adapted as you wish.

Lord: By my hand, by my will
I clear this place of all its ills
By my will, by my hand
I make a sacred place of this land.
HP: With earth we learn a new way
With the wind we sing a new day
With the fire we burn to survive
With water we respect our lives

Hail and welcome to the elements of our world.

All: Hail and welcome!

HP: I draw a circle of power in this consecrated space

Above me, below me, around me

Through objects and earth and air

This circle is formed in strength and wisdom

With the elements of all, and the presence of the Divine

By my Will, this circle is cast

So mote it be.

All: So mote it be!

HP: We all come from the Goddess

And to her we shall return

Like a drop of rain

Ever flowing to the ocean

We ask that you now join with us

Impart your wisdom and your grace

Passion and fertility now speak

To all that gather in this space.

All: Blessed be the Goddess!

HP: We all come from the Green God

And to him we shall return

Within the woodland creatures

And the winter fires burn

We ask that you now join with us

Impart your life philosophy

The heat and the hunter rises up

For all that stand and call to thee

All: Blessed be the God!

HP: We gather today as a circle of kith and kin

To honor the young man that stands within

Raise your voices for (state young lord's name)!

All to cheer, stamp feet and clap hands.

HP: A child once walked before us, holding hands for security and reassurance

Now a man walks in our stead, and the time has come to let go

Your time has come to walk unaided into the world

To make decisions based on the experiences of your youth

To accept the consequences of your actions

To take responsibility for your choices

To know that even as you walk into the world of adults

That every adult is still a child forever learning

It is with grief we say farewell to the child that once was

For the time seems to pass too quickly

And it is with joy we greet the man before us

Knowing that we still have many years together as a tribe, as a clan, as a family

We are honored to have been the ones chosen to support your youth

And we would be honored to support your journey into adulthood

This is the last time as a child that we lift you up

And the first time as an adult that we let you go your own way

With pride

With blessing

We acknowledge you as a man in your own right

So mote it be.

All: So mote it be!

At this point members of the circle will raise the young lord onto their shoulders and carry him deosil around the circle. If both men and women are participating in this rite, it is traditional for the women to raise the young lord and pass him to the men, symbolizing his movement from his mother's arms to his father's side.

HP: In the tradition of wisdom, father to son, we offer you the benefit of our life experiences. Many of us have stories to share, tales to tell, insights to offer and blessings to bestow. Let us break bread together, man to man, and share in the ceremony of our ancestors.

HP: From the sun to the corn
From the corn to the flour
From the flour to the bread
May we be blessed by this bounty
May we never hunger
We consecrate this bread in the name of the Masculine Divine
Eat and be merry.

At this point the bread is passed around the circle, a piece broken off for each member. As the bread is passed from hand to hand, the blessing of "Eat and be merry" should be spoken by the giver to the receiver.

HP: From the rain to the flowers
From the flowers to the bees
From the bees to the honey
From the honey to the mead
May we be blessed by this bounty
May we never thirst
We consecrate this mead in the name of the Feminine Divine
Drink and be merry.

At this point the mead horn is passed around the circle, each member taking a drink. As the mead horn is passed from hand to hand, the blessing of "Drink and be merry" should be spoken by the giver to the receiver.

HP: Young lord, child no more, sit, eat, drink and be merry whilst we give you the gift of knowledge gained by our own journeys into the world of man.

At this point food and drink should be shared and any circle member who wishes to participate should offer a few words of wisdom to the young lord. If anyone wishes to share physical gifts, this would also be an appropriate time to do so.

HP: We gathered, we celebrated, and together as kith and kin we have witnessed the child before us become a man among men. Today was a day to remember, and a tale to tell your descendants. Once more I ask you all to raise your voices for our young lord (speak young lord's name)!

All to cheer, stamp feet and clap hands.

HP: The time has come to depart, together let us say farewell.
HP: Blessed be the gracious Goddess
Mother of all, to whom we shall return
We thank you for blessing our gathering with your presence
In gratitude we say hail and farewell.
All: Hail and farewell!
HP: Blessed be the Green God
Father of all, to whom we shall return
We thank you for blessing our gathering with your presence
In gratitude we say hail and farewell.
All: Hail and farewell!
HP: With earth we learned a new way
With the wind we sang in a new day
With the fire we burned to survive
With water we respected our lives
Hail and farewell to the elements of our world
All: Hail and farewell!
HP: Let us carry this celebration in our hearts,
As our rite ends and we now depart
Bid fond farewell as the circle wanes
Merry met, merry part, merry we meet again.

All: Merry meet!
Merry part!
Merry meet again!

Rite of Passage – Mother and Father

My original intention for this chapter was to provide a wide array of sample ceremonies for all occasions. A rite of passage that many of us will experience at some point of our lives is that of stepping into the role of mother or father. For some, this shift is based upon age or experience, but for many this is the physical shift of becoming a parent. There are some beautiful rituals available to honor such a transition, but after some meditation on the matter I have decided not to include a formal ritual within these pages. From my own experiences of this powerful transition I must speak my truth and say that a formal ritual would have been overwhelming at an already overwhelming time of life.

Becoming a parent challenges everything you know, opens floodgates of emotions, and wears heavily upon the physical body. Since a life rite is about honoring the transitions of life, I would suggest that the best way to honor a new mother or father is by providing what they need to feel happy, healthy and whole. If what they need is a formal ritual among their spiritual support network, then by all means please do use the inspiration within these pages to create something unique and special. If what they need is help and support, then provide that with full under-standing of the spiritual, mental, and emotional impact it carries. If what they require is cleaning, cooking, someone to hold the baby whilst they bathe, or a shoulder to cry on, then provide that as an act of love and compassion.

So how can we make such mundane acts sacred? Simply by understanding that all acts of love and compassion are sacred. Make meals to keep them healthy and well nourished, knowing that you are providing the bounty of nature. Make a ritual of food preparation, use sacred herbs, stir in positivity and good health, and bless the food. Clean their home knowing that you not only cleanse their space and lighten their burden, but you also provide time for them to adjust to the transition. Offer to watch the baby whilst they take a hot bath, knowing that you are offering time for them to ease their bodies, calm their minds, and wash away their troubles. Be a shoulder to cry on if they so wish, for in doing so you are honoring who they are in raw, authentic truth without judgment or expectations. Be aware of the power of your words, for sometimes even the most well intentioned and commonly used phrases can have a negative energetic impact. For example, telling someone to enjoy every minute whilst they are tired and emotionally overwhelmed can make them feel like their emotions and experiences are not valid. Telling a new mother struggling with Birth Trauma that "the only thing that matters is a happy, healthy baby", implies that a happy, healthy mama is not important and that they are worthless, or worse, that they would somehow be willing to trade the health and wellbeing of their child for their own. Never forget that the words we use have the power to hurt or heal. There are so many ways that we can honor a person who is stepping into a new role, and sometimes the most traditional of rituals is not the most appropriate method. Sometimes it is these smallest of sacred acts, the kindness and compassion we display, that creates the largest impact.

Gentle Rebirthing of a Baby

With thoughts of Birth Trauma, a rather unspoken about but unfortunately frequent experience for many women, there are some small rituals that can greatly benefit the health and wellbeing of both parents and child. Birth Trauma does not just refer to physical difficulties related to birth, but also to the mental, emotional and spiritual challenges that an undesirable birth experience manifests. From depression and anxiety, to breast feeding troubles, Birth Trauma can impact a whole host of supposedly normal aspects of parenting. A Gentle Rebirthing

Ritual can greatly enhance the transition into parenting, especially when the initial impact of birthing is traumatic.

The technique is simple, and involves little more than a warm bath. The bath may be sprinkled with herbs and flowers, but please choose these wisely as the baby will also be present and some essential oils, herbs and flowers are not beneficial to young bodies without developed immune systems. Mother and child are situated in the bath, and the family has the opportunity to review any trauma or issues that the original birthing experience created. Once these feelings are acknowledged, the child can be lowered into the bath between the mother's legs, being careful to wet their scalp without submerging their face. The family then has the opportunity to experience a rebirth as the child is raised from between the mother's legs and placed upon her chest. Many babies will utter a short newborn cry, as if the process of moving from water to air holds a biological memory – regardless of the process in which they first experienced birth. This simple, gentle technique requires little preparation and no script, but the impact of such a ritual is profound. The chance to explore and let go of the feelings associated with Birth Trauma, whilst creating new memories of a pleasant rebirthing experience, can bring a sense of spiritual balance to the entire family.

Maybe after a period of adjustment to the role of mother or father, they will want a formal ritual to acknowledge the incredible new phase of life they have walked into. Support your loved ones in designing a ritual that is truly as unique and special as they are. Celebrate their journey in front of Gods, guides, kith and kin. Celebrate in quiet contemplation. Celebrate in laughter and dance. Celebrate the sacred.

Handfasting / Wedding Ceremony

Some Pagan paths acknowledge a two-stage process of Handfasting. The first stage is betrothal, a year and a day of energetic binding much like an engagement. The second stage is a formal Handfasting, a wedding where hands are literally and metaphorically tied together with Handfasting cords – the process from which we acquired the term "tying the knot". A Handfasting is usually phrased as a union for "as long as love shall last", rather than "until death do we part". This terminology allows for the uniqueness of relationships, from love that grows and changes, love that fades, love that lasts beyond death and love that lasts over many lifetimes.

By accepting that love may not last, we allow for a separation or divorce without breaking any vows, magically disrupting a binding, or psychologically enforcing a couple to remain in an unhealthy, unhappy relationship. Handfastings are not always a legal right within many countries, and instead many couples undergo a civil ceremony or legal wedding prior to a Handfasting in order to have their day of union legally acknowledged.

Handfastings are a form of magical binding, the tying together of people who love each other in a sacred union. Most Pagan paths are accepting and open of all sexualities, and Handfastings are not restricted to heterosexual couples. Handfastings have also become a popular option for those looking for an alternative to traditional church weddings and non-religious civil ceremonies, and are used by couples who have different spiritual or atheist beliefs.

At its core, a Handfasting is a declaration of love, a physical, emotional, mental and energetic commitment to your partner, and a life rite that acknowledges the sacredness of a loving relationship. This enables a Handfasting to be as unique and special as each relationship. Handfastings also offer a lot of variety within the rite, allowing a ritual to be tailored to each couple's beliefs. The following ritual is just one example of how a Handfasting may be performed, but each Handfasting can be designed specifically for the individuals involved.

Since many Handfastings are public ceremonies that include friends and family who may not follow the same spiritual path, it is quite common to see Handfastings that do not include any form of circle casting. Traditional wedding elements are often incorporated, usually with a magical twist; for example flower girls sprinkle a combination of flowers, herbs and salt to consecrate the space, and bridesmaids are transformed into handmaidens who represent the elements. Friends and family may be encouraged to sit in a circle, with the altar in the center, creating a natural boundary of love. There are many options to create wonderful, magical and inspiring ceremonies, so you are only limited by your imagination. I hope this following rite inspires your own creative ceremony.

The space is created with an altar at the center of a circle of chairs. An aisle is created from the south of the circle to the center, the position of love and passion and transformation. Guests are encouraged to be seated and comfortable. The Celebrant (HPS) calls for attention and welcomes the guests.

HPS: Welcome to you all, I have the honor today of officiating the Handfasting of (BRIDE) and (GROOM), in the presence of you, their family and friends, and in the presence of the ancestors and the Gods.

A Handfasting is a ceremony for, and the celebration of, the joining of two people who choose to devote their life and love to one another. This ceremony has been personally created to reflect their spiritual views and outlook on love and marriage. (BRIDE) and (GROOM) have written all the vows in today's ceremony themselves, so the words come from their hearts in truth and in love.

In this beautiful environment, we will witness and participate in the declaration of love that (BRIDE) and (GROOM) will make to each other. At this time, in this place, you are witnessing the time-old and sacred act of bonding, which transforms this place into a sacred space, blessed and holy.

Would the Groom and Best Man please step forward?

Groom and Best Man enter the circle and stand to the right of the Celebrant.

HPS: Would the Bride and her Handmaidens please step forward?

The Flower Girl enters scattering a mix of flowers, herbs and salt, followed by the Elemental Handmaidens and the Bride. The Elemental Handmaidens stand either side of the altar, Earth and Air on the right, Fire and Water on the left. The Bride stands to the left of the Celebrant, facing the Groom.
The Celebrant lights a white candle on the altar.

HPS: As I light this flame, may its light cast out all doubt and shadow from this place. May this light represent hope, love and the warmth of kinship.

The Bride lights a candle for Divinity.

Bride: I light a candle for our deities, for the polarity of Divinity, for the Lord and Lady in whom we believe.

The Groom lights a candle for the ancestors

Groom: I light a candle for history and family, for all those who came before us, for without whom we would not be.

HPS: Now in this beautiful location filled with family and friends we will join together the two who wish to be Handfasted. Who comes here this day?

The Bride states her name.

HPS: Who brings you here this day?
Bride: None but myself.
HPS: Why do you come here this day?
Bride: To declare my love for (GROOM).
HPS: Who comes here this day?

The Groom states his name.

HPS: Who brings you here this day?
Groom: None but myself.
HPS: Why do you come here this day?
Groom: To declare my love for (BRIDE).

The Celebrant cuts an apple horizontally to reveal the star within, one half given to the Bride, one half to the Groom.

HPS: As the stars of the sky appear within the fruit of the tree, so you will be the fruit that feeds each other and the star that guides you home to one another.
Bride and Groom: So we will.

The Bride and Groom both take a bite from the apple and replace the halves upon the offering plate.
The Celebrant pours a chalice of wine, mead or apple juice.

HPS: As the fruits of the earth are transformed into the drink of celebration, so shall the fruits of your marriage be transformed into many reasons to celebrate.

Bride and Groom: So it shall.

The Bride and Groom both take a sip from the chalice and return it to the Celebrant.

HPS: Does the Best Man have the rings?

The Best Man offers the wedding rings, either threaded onto the Handfasting cords or a wand.

HPS: (BRIDE) as you give this ring to (GROOM), remember that it is a symbol of your unity. The circle has no beginning and no end, and symbolizes the natural ever returning cycle of life. When (GROOM) looks upon this ring and knows your feelings, he will always be reminded of this day and the vows that you make. Do you offer this ring as a token of your love?

Bride: I do.

The Bride places the ring upon the Groom's finger.

HPS: (GROOM) as you give this ring to (BRIDE), remember that it is a symbol of your unity. The circle has no beginning and no end, and symbolizes the natural ever returning cycle of life. When (BRIDE) looks upon this ring and knows your feelings, she will always be reminded of this day and the vows that you make. Do you offer this ring as a token of your love?

Groom: I do.

The Groom places the ring upon the Bride's finger.

HPS: (BRIDE) and (GROOM), do you have anything you wish to say to each other in light of this day and the love you are

declaring?
Bride and Groom: We do.

At this point both the Bride and Groom will have the opportunity to declare their love and make their vows. This is highly personal and unique to each person. Speak from the heart.

Sample Vows
Husband/Wife to be,

I promise that you can depend on me, without losing your independence. I promise that we will spend quality time together, and quality time apart. I promise to honor you for who you are, and who you wish to be. I promise to support and share your dreams, as you have supported and shared mine. I promise to believe in you, even when you doubt yourself. I promise to kiss away your tears and share in your smiles. I promise to stand by your side and sleep in your arms. I promise to be all that I can be for you, your lover, your friend, and the father/mother of our children. Husband/wife to be, from this day forward, for as long as love shall last, I promise to be your wife/husband.

The Celebrant binds the Bride and Groom's hands together with woven Handfasting cords. The color of these cords can reflect the qualities that the couple desire for their union.

HPS: Today in the presence of kith and kin, ancestors and deities, you have spoken of your bond to one another, the bond of friendship and of love. As I symbolize this bond by binding your hands in the old tradition of Handfasting, I offer you both these words of wisdom:

Above you are the stars, below you the stones. As time does pass remember; like a star should your love be constant, even when not on show. Like a stone should your love be firm, yet smooth with the passage of time. Be close, yet not too close, for the cypress will not grow in the shadow of the oak. Possess one another, yet be understanding of each other's freedom. Have patience with one another, for storms will come but they will pass quickly. Be free in giving of affection and warmth. Hold hands often, and be passionate and sensuous to one another. Have no fear, and let not the ways or the words of others give you unease, for the two of you will support each other, now and always.

The Celebrant presents the Bride and Groom to the Elemental Handmaidens for blessings.

HPS: I present (BRIDE) and (GROOM) in their sacred union; do you have a gift of wisdom for them?

Earth: As I stand for North and Earth, I feel inspired to gift you both with stability and fertility. May you always find your way home to one another, and may your lives grow and flourish in the garden of your dreams.

HPS: I present (BRIDE) and (GROOM) in their sacred union; do you have a gift of wisdom for them?

Air: As I stand for East and Air, I feel inspired to gift you both with inspiration and communication. May you always face each dawn with a kiss, and may your wonderful life together be a story told to your children's children.

HPS: I present (BRIDE) and (GROOM) in their sacred union; do you have a gift of wisdom for them?

Fire: As I stand for South and Fire, I feel inspired to gift you both with passion and love. May you hold hands as young lovers do, even in your twilight days, and may your lives be filled with the sunshine of each other's smiles.

HPS: I present (BRIDE) and (GROOM) in their sacred union; do you have a gift of wisdom for them?

Water: As I stand for West and Water, I feel inspired to gift you both with transformation and understanding. May you support each other as you grow and change, and may your life flow smoothly around any obstacles you face together.

HPS: As (GROOM) is to the masculine, so (BRIDE) is to the feminine, for what one lacks, the other may give. There is no greater gift to give than that of your love. Blessed be your union!

The Bride and Groom may now kiss to seal their vows.

The Bride and Groom kiss.

HPS: With this blessing, (BRIDE) and (GROOM) are now married as husband and wife in the eyes of kith and kin, ancestors and Gods. Stand with me to honor their union. Blessed Be!

All: Blessed be!

HPS: The sharing of food and drink with kith and kin in celebration is a time-honored tradition. It is the forerunner of the Wedding Feast, and today is no different. We may now eat and drink a little, and in doing so, we will share in the love and good fortune of (BRIDE) and (GROOM). Eat, drink and be merry. This Handfasting is complete. So mote it be!

All: So mote it be!

Handparting (Divorce / Separation) Rite

A Handparting rite is a Pagan divorce. Divorce is not frowned upon within most Pagan paths, as it is accepted that people do grow and change as individuals, which may impact the relationship. In some cases the best thing to do to avoid harm is to make the decision to cut the cords that bind a couple together and move forward as individuals.

A handparting is not completed until both parties come to an agreement about division of belongings and resolve any custody issues. A High Priest or Priestess may support this process, but it is advised that people seek professional support through legal channels and counseling services. Once the couple have sought all the support they need to finalize the legal aspect of their separation, and are both in agreement that this is the best course of action, a High Priest or Priestess can officiate a rite to acknowledge this separation and assist in removing any energetic ties that remain between the couple.

HPS: As I sweep the circle in to out
May the besom clear our path ahead
Sweep away the negativity
Leave room for peace instead.

The HPS smudges each participant.

HPS: Lighter than air
Troubles rise
From earth to the skies
Be free, at peace
A mind at rest
Blessed
By Earth's regeneration

By sweeping rushing Air
By the cleansing Fire
By purity of Water
I manifest a sacred place
Of hope and healing
Take form
By my will
So mote it be.
All: So mote it be.
HPS: Blessed Goddess, we call to thee
Blessed God, hear our plea
We seek your strength and wisdom
For this rite of parting and freedom
In unique divinity and in sacred union
We ask for perspective in times to come
Please lend us your insight and grace
For the rite held within sacred space
With blessings we receive the Divine
In this time outside of time
Blessed Goddess, hail and welcome.
All: Blessed Goddess, hail and welcome.
HPS: Blessed God, hail and welcome.
All: Blessed God, hail and welcome.
HPS: Today we gather together to witness the Handparting of (Partner 1) and (Partner 2). May you both find release and peace from this process. (Partner 1) please step forward. Who brings you here this day?
Partner 1: None but myself.
HPS: Why do you come here this day?
Partner 1: To release myself and (Partner 2) from the bonds of our Handfasting.
HPS: Do you bring friends or family to support you in this decision?
Partner 1: I do bring support.

HPS: (Partner 2) please step forward. Who brings you here this day?

Partner 2: None but myself.

HPS: Why do you come here this day?

Partner 2: To release myself and (Partner 1) from the bonds of our Handfasting.

HPS: Do you bring friends or family to support you in this decision?

Partner 2: I do bring support.

HPS: You are both in agreement that you wish to end your union and take new paths?

Both Partners: We are.

HPS: Have you reached agreements on the physical division of shared belongings, shared responsibility of any outstanding debts, and resolved any issues regarding the shared care and responsibility of any family or pets affected by your decision?

Both Partners: We have agreed to ___ (list the agreements and terms of separation here. Any disagreements can be resolved within circle, or the rite can be postponed until an agreement can be reached).

HPS: Once you walked the same path, but now that path separates and travels in different directions. You both stand at a crossroads and face an uncertain future, but you must be certain of this first step. Today you both make the decision to cut the ties that bind each other, so that you may both move forward with free will and forgiveness wherever your new paths take you. These cords from your Handfasting rite symbolize the union you have shared. In order to cut your ties to each other, you must first cut these cords. No one can do this for you, it is a step you must take yourselves. If you would both take a blade, please take a moment to reflect upon all the good days, good times and good experiences you shared together. Allow the negativity, the stress, and the memories of bad days to flow out of you into the Earth and keep just the positive thoughts in your mind. In this frame of positivity, you may cut the cords without animosity.

Both partners take part in cutting through the cords

HPS: (Partner 1) and (Partner 2) you have now released each other from the bonds of your Handfasting. This day marks the ending of one chapter of your life, and the beginning of a new chapter. May you both take on board the lessons of your past to create a beautiful future life for yourselves. Do you vow to walk into the future with free will, freedom from the past, and if possible, forgiveness in your hearts?

Partner 1: I free myself and (Partner 2) from the past union. I forgive myself and (Partner 2) for the difficulties that led to this day. I exercise my free will to create a new future for myself.

Partner 2: I free myself and (Partner 1) from the past union. I forgive myself and (Partner 1) for the difficulties that led to this day. I exercise my free will to create a new future for myself.

The cut cords may be burned at this point if both participants wish to do so.

HPS: I declare this rite of parting complete. Please return to your support networks. May each of you remember the agreements that you made this day, and face the future with hope, healing, forgiveness and strength. So mote it be.

All: So mote it be.

HPS: Blessed Goddess, Blessed God,
We thank you for your strength and insight
During this couple's Handparting rite
Go if you wish, stay if you will

Blessed be.

All: Blessed be.

HPS: Earth of new growth

Air of changing winds

Fire of transformation

Water of turning tides

We thank you for your presence in this rite

Go if you wish, stay if you will

Blessed be.

All: Blessed be.

HPS: Blessed circle, purpose fulfilled

I release thee now, by my Will

Circle open, never broken

So mote it be.

All: So mote it be.

HPS: I would like to thank all the participants of this rite, seen and unseen, for their presence. Thank you to each and every participant who displayed such strength, support and love. May we all reflect upon the past that shapes us, and the future that we shape each day. Blessings to you all.

Croning Ceremony

A Croning Ceremony marks the life transition into our twilight years, a phase of life that is related to age and wisdom. For many women, a Croning is performed after menopause, when they become a grandmother, or between the ages of 50 and 60. However, there is so much variety of life experiences and physical changes that the age of a woman who feels she is entering her Crone stage may range dramatically.

Claiming the title of Crone is a form of reclaiming personal power in a society that appears to devalue age. The image of the ugly old hag, unloved and unwanted, is now being replaced by active women of confidence and power who celebrate the freedom that age brings. The wisdom and life experience of our elders is honored during this ceremony. Much like the life rite that honors the transition of child to young woman, the Croning ritual is usually an all-women affair. However, there is no reason why this must be so, should the woman being Croned wish for the input and experience of her male friends and family. Croning ceremonies are much more common than their masculine counterpart, the Saging Ceremony, but the process is very similar. At its core a Croning or Saging Ceremony is a life rite to honor the transformation, wisdom and experience that age brings. This ritual is about dignity and honor, and respecting the elders in our community.

The following ritual is an all-female-based Croning Ceremony, since this is the most commonly requested ceremony related to age, but the format and language can certainly inspire a Saging Ceremony by simply focusing on what age and wisdom means to the masculine elder. You can also use this ritual as a foundation for creating a nonspecific Eldering Ceremony. Although it is traditional for a High Priestess to officiate the rite, I have seen some beautiful ceremonies where each woman present took equal energetic responsibility and leadership. This example blends a High Priestess with the wisdom of Elders representing Earth, Air, Fire and Water.

Women gather together to honor the woman who is to be Croned. The altar may contain pictures of loved ones since passed over and inspirational woman (known or unknown), as well as the usual ritual items. It is common for the altar cloth and candles to be black or purple in representation of the Crone. In the North of the circle the Elemental Elders form an arch with their hands, each participant walking under the arch to enter the circle. Each participant is greeted as they walk under the arch.

Elders: You were born of a woman, and of women you are born again into this circle.

HPS: Today we gather, woman to woman, to honor the cycle of life and the presence of the Crone. As I light this candle, may its light chase away the shadows of doubt and insecurity. May this be a sacred space of power, a place of peace, and an environment of inspiration and honor.

Elders: Please hold hands and form the circle of unity.

Air Elder: The rushing winds form this circle. The spring of our youth forms this circle. The whispered wisdom forms this circle. The breath of woman forms this circle.

Fire Elder: The flames of transformation form this circle. The summer of life forms this circle. The passion of living forms this circle. The heat of our bodies form this circle.

Water Elder: The rivers of belief form this circle. The autumn of our maturity forms this circle. The ebb and flow of energy forms this circle. The joy and sadness of our tears form this circle.

Earth Elder: The cycle of life, death and rebirth forms this circle. The winter of our life forms this circle. The shadow of the Crone forms this circle. The power and presence of woman forms this circle.

HPS: As the energy moves from hand to hand, we create a sacred space of this land. The circle is cast from woman to woman, as within, so without, as above so below. So mote it be.

All: The circle is cast. So mote it be.

HPS: In times past, a woman who lived to be a Crone was considered an elder of the community, a wise woman, an honored woman. In current days, too often women are shamed and devalued as they age. It is time to reclaim the power of the Crone, to honor ourselves, to honor our wisdom, experience, strength and ability. Today we honor one among us who steps into the position of the Crone, and as such it is only fitting that she should be the one to call forth the power of the Crone. Let her speak now and awaken the Crone without and the Crone within.

One of the participants should offer the Crone Initiate a black or purple shawl to symbolize being enveloped by the Crone's power.

Crone Initiate: I am the beauty of dark moon, of dark night, of dusk and twilight, of the long evening of your life.

I am the dark earth beneath your feet, from which all is born and all returns eventually.

I am the flesh and bone, worn well and aged to perfection.

I am courage, freedom, truth and wisdom found in every life lived in honor.

I am transition, rebirth and midwife to the dying.

I was with you at the beginning, and I was the wisdom of elders during your youth.

I will be with you at the end and beyond.

I am Crone, reclaiming the power of age.

I am Crone.

All: We are the Crone!

HPS: Is there anything you would like to share with us about your journey, any thoughts and feelings you have on reclaiming the power of the Crone?

The Crone Initiate may speak from the heart or offer a reading that reflects her feelings.

HPS: Many here are elders of our community, and some are still walking in the sunshine of their youth. We are women of wisdom and experience, women of passion and inspiration, women supporting women. Is there anyone here who wishes to offer their insight and blessings?

The women may all have their chance to offer wisdom and advice, or share a story. This community sharing usually starts with the oldest woman present, giving the first voice and position of respect to the oldest Crone participating. Other groups may wish to work widdershins around the circle, representing the waning of life and the power of the Old Goddess.

HPS: The Crone is among us, the Crone is around us, the Crone is within us. We walk among the Crones of the world, and we are the Crones of the world. We walk with history and experience on our side, and with the knowledge that our journey of learning is eternal. We must learn now to embody the Crone, to be the Crone, to bear the power and peace of the Crone. Let us offer our gifts to our new Crone, and in doing so we will honor our Spiritual Sister, we will honor ourselves, we will honor our ancestors, and we will honor all that it means to be Crone.

Participants provide small tokens or trinkets that can be tied to a staff. This staff represents the support of a community of women, whilst also representing the independence and self-reliance of the individual woman. After the gift giving, a simple song or chant whilst holding hands affirms the sisterhood of women everywhere.

Suggested Chant:
I am she and she is me
Woman to woman, forever known
I am she and she is me
Maiden, Mistress, Priestess, Crone.

HPS: We call to the Crone, within and without. We honor your presence here on this blessed occasion. In love we bid you farewell, yet understand you cannot leave that which you exist within. We each carry the power of the Crone within us, at all times. Goddess within, we thank thee. Goddess without, we honor thee. Blessed be.

All: Goddess within, we thank thee. Goddess without, we honor thee. Blessed be!

Water Elder: By blood and tears, heart and soul, we release this circle. May it flow back into the universe, leaving nothing but love in its wake.

Fire Elder: By power and passion, desire and drive, we release this circle. May it scatter back into the universe, leaving nothing but the light of love behind.

Air Elder: By breath and thought, knowledge and inspiration, we release this circle. May it rush back into the universe, leaving nothing but the echoes of love.

Earth Elder: By flesh and bone, strength and will, we release this circle. May it sink back into the universe, leaving nothing but a love that grows.

All: Hand to hand, woman to woman
The rite is complete, the circle open.

HPS: Woman to woman, child to Crone
We claim the power as our own
With love eternal filling each heart
Merry we meet and merry we part.

All: Merry meet, merry part, merry meet again!

Last Rites / Passing Over Ritual

There are not many rites specifically designed for attending the dying at the point of their passing. This ritual has been designed for simplicity and brevity, should time be of the essence. The dying may not be able to communicate during their passing, so this rite has been designed to be a blessing from the High Priest or Priestess without expectation of input. The rite can easily be adapted to include participation from the dying, their friends or family. As with all rites, this is an energetic ritual, a way of raising and releasing energy to assist a soul as it transitions from one life to the next.

HP/S: As above, 'tis so below
As the Universe, so the soul
As within, 'tis so without
Circle raised, cast about

The wheel of the world turns, Earth blesses you
The winds of change whisper, Air blesses you
The flame of love burns bright, Fire blesses you
The river flows to the sea, Water blesses you
The Divine calls your name, Spirit blesses you

Blessed Gods, I bid you come
This soul needs guiding home

Include the following or similar blessing only if it feels appropriate at the time:

Dearest Beloved, you are not alone
I am here to help guide you home
If your soul is ready now to depart

Then leave without a heavy heart
With forgiveness and without fear
For those you love will hold you dear

Use this chant to focus your intention if you wish, or as a way of involving family or friends energetically:

As below, 'tis so above
You are not alone
You are loved
You are loved
You are loved

Upon passing over:

Farewell friend, may love light your way
You live on in the hearts of those who love you
In the minds of those who remember you
And on the breath of those who speak your name
What is remembered, lives

Be free, at peace,
At rest, at ease
There is no reason to remain tied to this earthly plane
This circle will stay with you until you find your way
May your ancestors take you by the hand
May the Gods welcome you into the Summerlands
So mote it be.

Requiem Rite

In this Requiem Rite, otherwise known as a funeral service, I have used the term "Our Beloved" to refer to the deceased loved one. This may of course be replaced with their birth name, craft name or nickname as the mourners wish. When casting a circle for funeral purposes, it is common practice to call to the quarters and cast the sacred space widdershins, representing the journey that starts with an ending, the returning journey to the earth and the inner journey of the bereaved. As such, the closing of the circle would be completed deosil, ending in the west where the rite started.

HP: I cleanse this space of past conflicts and prepare the way for united hearts. May this space be sacred and safe for both living and departed. May we all find peace within the boundaries of this circle.

HPS: I cast about this space and all within
A circle of peace and love and honor.
May the energies of the earth encircle us
As the circle of life and death reveals itself
This space is not a place
In a time outside of time
At a point between the worlds of the living
And those who reside beyond the veil.
So mote it be.

All: So mote it be.

WQ: Our tears like the salt waters of the oceans ebb and flow, our hearts spill with emotion. We seek the blessing of water's presence, to lend clarity, honesty, and healing to this rite. Find home in our hearts, comfort in our tears, and love within our grief. Be with us in our hour of need. Blessed be.

All: Blessed be.

SQ: As the sun sets upon the day and darkness falls, so does a light leave our lives with the passing of Our Beloved. We seek the blessings of fire to kindle old memories to burn bright, to scatter the embers of love into each heart and warm us in the cold dark nights of grief. Find a home in our hearts, comfort in our community, and love within our grief. Be with us in our hour of need. Blessed be.

All: Blessed be.

EQ: As the breath of life leaves Our Beloved and whispers out into the universe, so do we whisper our words of love and loss, gratitude and grief out into the universe. We seek the blessings of Air to communicate our thoughts and feelings, our hopes and dreams, beyond this space and into the realms of spirit. Find a home in our hearts, comfort in our words, and love within our grief. Be with us in our hour of need. Blessed be.

All: Blessed be.

NQ: As the earth blesses us with the cycles of life and death, so do we celebrate the life and mourn the death of Our Beloved. We seek the blessings of earth to bring under-standing of life and death, to welcome Our Beloved back to the earth, and to lend us the strength to endure our grief. Find a home in our hearts, comfort in our remembrance, and love within our grief. Be with us in our hour of need. Blessed be.

All: Blessed be.

Drawing down of the Moon and Sun:

HP: You are the Goddess of all, as are all women, the mother of birth and death, of womb and tomb; the mother of cycles and seasons, the mother of transition and transformations, beginnings and endings. I reach out to you now, the Feminine Divine, to be present in our rite of love and loss. Share with us your strength, compassion and understanding.

All: Hail and welcome.

HPS: You are the God of all, as are all men, the father of life and death, the father of cycles and seasons, the father of harvest, hunt and sacrifice. I reach out to you now, the Masculine Divine, to be present in our rite of love and loss. Share with us your strength, compassion and understanding.

All: Hail and welcome.

HP: We gather here today in a circle of love and trust between All that is seen and yet unseen
To mourn the passing of one who has touched hearts and minds
To celebrate with joy the wonder of their life.

HPS: To hold hands and hearts, hearts and hands
As united in grief and love we stand
We bid farewell to a dear soul who journeys far from us
Leaving physical form and returning to star dust.

HP: We understand the cycle of birth and death
And know that their energy never ends
It scatters out into our universe, the dancing spiral
A part of all that was and remains eternal.

HPS: With their love upon us, and our love upon them,
We know that we must part ways with our dear friend.
We are touched and forever changed by a life lived so well
On this day we simply say hail and farewell…

All: Hail and farewell.

HPS: Our Beloved has died and left this physical plane. No one who has passed should leave this world without knowing the love felt by friends and family, kith and kin. May our love and loss ease the transition from this life to the next for both Our Beloved and ourselves. We offer our love to light the way in dark days and nights to come.

All: We offer love to light the way in darkness.

HP: One life touches many others, and many others impact just one life. We are a web of connection, in this life and beyond. No one should pass from this place without knowing the impact of their life upon friends and family, kith and kin. May our celebration of life, mourning of death and honor of existence ease the transition from this life for both Our Beloved and for ourselves. We honor this life, and our own.

All: We honor life and the connections of life.

HPS: Our Beloved, we light this candle for you, for the light of your life continues to burn brightly in the hearts and minds of those who miss you. The light of your soul continues to burn bright in the memories of this life and in the worlds beyond.

HP: At this time, let us all have the opportunity to offer our words of love, of comfort, of celebration of a life lived well. If anyone does not wish to share words, but wishes to leave a token, please feel free to do so.

WQ: By the gifts of water may our tears cleanse our hearts of grief, and may our emotions of love and gratitude carry Our Beloved gently into the Summerlands.

SQ: By the gifts of fire may our hearts be warmed by fond memories, and may the light of Our Beloved's soul burn bright in the Summerlands.

EQ: By the gifts of air may our lips whisper words of comfort, and may Our Beloved's soul rise and soar in the Summerlands.

NQ: By the gifts of earth may we accept the seasons and cycles of life and death, and may Our Beloved find comfort and peace in the arms of Mother Nature.

If you would like to include a cakes and ale rite as a part of the requiem rite, this would be an appropriate point to do so. I personally feel that this can more readily be incorporated into a traditional post funeral gathering where the sharing of food is a usual part of both Pagan and non-Pagan customs.

HP: Our Beloved, beyond last breath

Beyond life, beyond death

May the God guide you through your journey

May our love surround you as you travel.

HPS: Our Beloved, beyond pain and sorrow

Beyond today, beyond tomorrow

May the Goddess guide you through the transition from this life to the next.

HP: As the wheel turns, and the veil thins, we will honor you again at Samhain, as ancestor, as family, as beloved dead.

All: Blessed be.

NQ: From womb to tomb, beginnings to endings, the cycle of earth teaches us that all death is a transition upon an eternal journey. We thank the presence of North and Earth in our rite. Hail and farewell.

All: Hail and farewell.

EQ: May the stories of Our Beloved's life be told for many years to come. We thank the presence of East and Air in our rite. Hail and farewell.

All: Hail and farewell.

SQ: May the loving memories of Our Beloved burn bright for years to come. We thank the presence of South and Fire in our rite. Hail and farewell.

All: Hail and farewell.

WQ: The west is the direction of endings, yet every ending is a new beginning. We thank the presence of West and Water in our rite. Hail and farewell.

All: Hail and farewell.

HP: We thank the presence of the Divine in our rite. Please go if you must, stay if you will. Blessed be.

All: Blessed be.

HPS: We close this circle and send the energy back to nature, to seek its own balance and purpose within the Divine All. A circle open is never broken, just as a life departing does break the bonds of love. We hold Our Beloved in our hearts, if not in our arms, and we leave this sacred space of love and honor with gratitude that our lives have been forever changed by Our Beloved's presence. What is remembered, lives on.

All: What is remembered, lives on. So mote it be.

Samhain – 31st October / 1st November

Samhain, or Summer's End, is Celtic fire festival that has evolved into our modern day Halloween festival. It is both the last harvest festival and a celebration and honoring of the beloved dead. It is a time sacred to the Goddess as wise Crone, to the Goddess as Mother close to her time birthing the new God of Light, to the God of Shadows who rules the waning of the year, to the Holly King who rules until Winter Solstice, to the God as Hunter and to all the deities who descend into the Underworld during the winter months. The descent of the Goddess is retold in the stories of Inanna, Ishtar and Persephone.

The veil between the worlds is thin at this time of year, giving us an opportunity to see beyond and witness the secrets of life, death and rebirth. We can communicate with the spirits of our loved ones, and practice our divinatory arts and prophetic skills. On the physical realm, we harvest the last of the fruits, tend to the root vegetables and preserve and prepare the foods that are required during the winter months. For many Pagan paths, Samhain is the end of one year and the beginning of another and is often be seen as the appropriate time to rid ourselves of unwanted habits or behaviors. This festival is all about life, love and loss, and the variety of myths about this point in the Wheel of the Year provides a rich source of inspiration for Samhain celebrations.

As with all my sample rituals, I have chosen just one or two prevalent themes to work with and offer as an example. Rituals can highlight individual themes, or combine a variety of seasonal themes, dependant on the needs of the individual or group.

HPS: The wheel turns, as we turn
We spiral into darkness, deep and complete
Stripping away all to truth and bone

Clearing the way in one fell sweep.
HP: Divine darkness reigns
Prepare the descending way
For the Underworld is host
To sacred night and day.
HPS: I cast about this place
A circle veil thin
To straddle time and space
To honor all within
In every shifting plane
In all times and none
I cast a sacred space
From earth below to sky above
So mote it be.
All: So mote it be.
NQ: Hail to the element of North and Earth
Of mountains and valleys
Of forest and stone
Of bitter winter
Of hearth and home
We welcome your presence in our rite
As we gather upon this Samhain night
Hail and welcome.
All: Hail and welcome.
EQ: Hail to the element of East and Air
Of thought and voice
Of breeze and gale
Of flight and freedom
Of winter's wail
We welcome your presence in our rite
As we gather upon this Samhain night
Hail and welcome.
All: Hail and welcome.
SQ: Hail to the element of South and Fire

Of desire and love
Of rage and ire
Of burning sun
Of winter fires.
We welcome your presence in our rite
As we gather upon this Samhain night
Hail and welcome.
All: Hail and welcome.
WQ: Hail to the element of West and Water
Of raging river
Of quiet streams
Of frozen lakes
Of bitter sea
We welcome your presence in our rite
As we gather upon this Samhain night
Hail and welcome.
All: Hail and welcome.
HP: On this night we celebrate the spiral dance of life to death to new life. The wheel has turned, the harvest is home, the Crone turns her face towards us, and the Hunter rides the fields and forests. The veil thins, and spirits draw close to hearth and home. We welcome the transition from womb to tomb to womb, for the cycle of life tells us all that dies shall be reborn.
HPS: Dark Mother, Grandmother of time and tide,
We welcome you into our hearts and homes.
You have blessed us with your bounty, and now we reap the spiritual harvest that resides in the dark places of mind and soul.
With your wisdom to guide us, we seek to reveal the secrets of our deepest selves.
With your wisdom to guide us, we seek to honor our ancestors, our beloved dead, and our beloved living.
With your wisdom to guide us, we seek to find comfort and

celebration even in the darkest of days and nights.

Old Crone, midwife to the mother of the sun, be with us now as we usher in the new year.

All: Beloved Goddess, hail and welcome!

HP: Dark Lord, wild Hunter of the untamed places,

We welcome you into our hearts and homes.

You bless us in the winter months, and reveal the bounty of life to be found in the harshest of seasons.

With your wisdom to guide us, we seek understanding of our own wild nature.

With your wisdom to guide us, we seek to reveal the ebb and flow of energetic journeys.

With your wisdom to guide us, we seek strength, compassion, and Divine connection for even the darkest of days and nights.

Horned Hunter, seed of the new sun, be with us now as we usher in the new year.

All: Beloved God, hail and welcome!

HPS: Here lies the burning cauldron of transformation. May all who wish to rid themselves of past hurts and habits cast them now into the fire. With the death of the old, new life is born.

HP: With lightened hearts, we turn towards the spirits of land and sea, the spirits of life and death. May all who wish to do so, light a candle in memory of those gone but not forgotten.

HPS: With blessed candle, pure and white

I welcome the beloved dead this night

May those we seek follow this light

And those unwelcome turn from its sight.

All: Blessed be the Beloved Dead.

HP: From skies to the rains,

From the rains to the roots,

From the roots to the fruits,

From the fruits to the wine.

We consecrate and bless this wine in the name of the Lord of Shadows, the Dark Goddess, and the beloved dead.

Raise your cup in blessing of our bounty!

All: May we never thirst!

HPS: From the earth to the seed,

From the seed to the corn,

From the corn to the grain,

From the grain to the bread.

We consecrate and bless this bread in the name of the Lord of Shadows, the Dark Goddess, and the beloved dead.

Break your bread in blessing of our bounty!

All: May we never hunger!

HP: Blessed God, Hunter Divine,

We thank you for your presence this night

Go if you must, stay if you will

With gratitude we say hail and farewell.

All: Hail and farewell.

HPS: Blessed Goddess, Crone Divine,

We thank you for your presence this night

Go if you must, stay if you will

With gratitude we say hail and farewell.

All: Hail and farewell.

WQ: We bid farewell to the element of West and Water

We thank you for your presence this night

Go if you must, stay if you wish

Hail and farewell.

All: Hail and farewell.

SQ: We bid farewell to the element of South and Fire

We thank you for your presence this night

Go if you must, stay if you wish

Hail and farewell.

All: Hail and farewell.

EQ: We bid farewell to the element of East and Air

We thank you for your presence this night

Go if you must, stay if you wish

Hail and farewell.

All: Hail and farewell.

NQ: We bid farewell to the element of North and Earth

We thank you for your presence this night

Go if you must, stay if you wish

Hail and farewell.

All: Hail and farewell.

HPS: As we darken the flames of our bright circle

We know that their light still burns in the worlds beyond

May their spirit light our way in time of darkness

A ritual ended, but not forgotten

Merry met, merry part, merry shall we meet again.

HP: We thank all who attended the circle this night

All those seen and unseen who joined in this rite

Go if you must, stay if you will,

In fondness we say hail and farewell.

Yule / Winter Solstice – 21st / 22nd December

The Winter Solstice festival, sometimes referred to as Midwinter or Yule, is the point on the Wheel of the Year where the waning sun pauses and starts to wax again. The sun is reborn, and light starts to increase. The two most common themes for this festival are that of the birth of the new Sun God, often referred to as the Child of Promise, and the cyclical battle between the Holly and Oak Kings who fight for supremacy over the waxing half of the year. Although the Holly and Oak Kings are presented as distinct and separate entities, as with many aspects of the Divine they are also considered to be dual halves or mirror aspects of each other for one cannot be without the other.

The mythology of the new born Son (Sun) as a Child of Promise is reflected in many cultures across time. The celebration of increasing light within the darkness and cold of winter is a promise of future warmth, growth and prosperity. Many aspects of this winter festival have been incorporated into modern-day Christmas festivities, so it is not uncommon to find Pagan inspiration within the widely accepted practices and associations of Christmas celebrations – from gift giving, sharing of food and shelter, lighting of candles and sacred fires, decorations with greenery and the use of red and gold, to the mythology of a God that fathers an aspect of himself to bring hope to humanity. The underlying energy of this festival is light within darkness, and promise that increasing light brings to heart, mind and body.

HPS: I cast a circle of power above and below, inside and outside, around and about us
Strengthened by Earth,
Formed by Air,
Charged by Fire

Cleansed by Water
Consecrated by Spirit
As above, 'tis so below
This circle is cast
So mote it be.
All: So mote it be.
NQ: Hail to the element of North and Earth
Of mountains and valleys
Of forest and stone
Of bitter winter
Of hearth and home
We welcome your presence in our rite
As we gather upon this sacred night
Hail and welcome.
All: Hail and welcome.
EQ: Hail to the element of East and Air
Of thought and voice
Of breeze and gale
Of flight and freedom
Of winter's wail
We welcome your presence in our rite
As we gather upon this sacred night
Hail and welcome.
All: Hail and welcome.
SQ: Hail to the element of South and Fire
Of desire and love
Of rage and ire
Of burning sun
Of winter fires
We welcome your presence in our rite
As we gather upon this sacred night
Hail and welcome.
All: Hail and welcome.
WQ: Hail to the element of West and Water

Of raging river
Of quiet streams
Of frozen lakes
Of bitter sea
We welcome your presence in our rite
As we gather upon this sacred night
Hail and welcome.
All: Hail and welcome.
HP: We gather here today to celebrate the birth of the God and the rebirth of the sun. The reminder that even in the depths of winter, light grows stronger and chases away the shadows of hardship. With the shortest day and the longest night upon us, we can look towards the increasing light in hope, in promise of new growth, in promise of the future. The sun is our promise, and the son is the child of promise.
HPS: We gather here today to bring warmth to those who are cold, to share our bounty with those who have none, to bring love and joy to those who suffer in the depths of winter. As the earth is our mother, may we care for our kith and kin as any mother would, by bringing comfort in times of grief or isolation. This is a season of joy for many, and difficulty for some. Let us share in our abundance, as the promise of lighter days ahead.
HP: Hail to the God of light, the son and the Sun
As light spills across the land in promise of days to come
We celebrate your birth and rebirthing cycle
And welcome your presence here in our circle.
Hail and welcome!
All: Hail and welcome.
HPS: Hail to the Goddess of birth and death and rebirth.
Goddess as Mother, as Old Crone midwife, as winter earth
We celebrate your journey and seasonal cycle
And welcome your presence here in our circle
Hail and welcome!

All: Hail and welcome.

It is appropriate for each participant to light a candle at this point, and meditate upon the light that grows within the circle as each candle is lit.

HP: Hail to the sun of seasons
Striding bold across the father's skies
Hail to the sun of illumination
Banishing darkness on land and in mind
Hail to the sun of gentle touch
Shadows flee before your reaching rays
Hail to the sun of blessing
The kiss of the Divine on my upturned face,
All: Hail to the sun, light eternal!
HPS: Each little light is the light of our lives, individually we illuminate each other, together we illuminate the world. May we each be a bright light in the darkness, to uplift another's heart, to help someone find their way, to keep others warm. May we shine from within, so that others may recognize the light within themselves. At a time of want, need, and harsh winter, let us bring food, friendship, comfort and warmth to each other.

This is a great time to introduce a meditation on need and abundance, or to even hold a very practical and generous act of gathering food and clothing donations in the center of the circle. Items can be blessed or charged with energy before being distributed to those in need after the rite. Some groups will do sacrifice swaps at Yule, giving something that is personally precious to another participant for safe keeping in order to learn the art of sacrifice.

HP: As the athame is to the male.
HPS: So the chalice is to the female.

HP: For what one lacks, the other may give.

HPS: There is no greater power in the universe than that of love.

HP: From the sun to the corn

From the corn to the flour

From the flour to the bread

May we be blessed by this bounty

May we never hunger

We consecrate this bread in the name of the Lord and Lady

Eat and be merry.

Each participant to share in the giving and receiving of bread.

HPS: From the rain to the vine

From the vine to the fruit

From the fruit to the wine

May we be blessed by this bounty

May we never thirst

We consecrate this wine in the name of the Lord and Lady

Drink and be merry.

Each participant to share in the giving and receiving of wine.

HP: Blessed God, our Sun reborn,

We thank you for your presence in this rite

Go if you must, stay if you will

With gratitude we say hail and farewell.

All: Hail and farewell.

HPS: Blessed Goddess, Divine Mother,

We thank you for your presence in this rite

Go if you must, stay if you will

With gratitude we say hail and farewell.

All: Hail and farewell.

WQ: We bid farewell to the element of West and Water

We thank you for your presence this night
Go if you must, stay if you wish
Hail and farewell.
All: Hail and farewell.
SQ: We bid farewell to the element of South and Fire
We thank you for your presence this night
Go if you must, stay if you wish
Hail and farewell.
All: Hail and farewell.
EQ: We bid farewell to the element of East and Air
We thank you for your presence this night
Go if you must, stay if you wish
Hail and farewell.
All: Hail and farewell.
NQ: We bid farewell to the element of North and Earth
We thank you for your presence this night
Go if you must, stay if you wish
Hail and farewell.
All: Hail and farewell.
HPS: I draw back the energy of the circle
And send it down to our Mother Earth
The circle is released from purpose to be reborn again
As I will it, so mote it be.
All: So mote it be.
HP: We bless all those who have attended
And participated in this rite
May you carry the joy from this celebration
In your hearts for many a night.
All: Merry meet, merry part, merry meet again!

Imbolc Ritual – 1st / 2nd February

Imbolc, otherwise called Oimlich or Candlemas, is a festival on the cusp of winter and spring sacred to the Goddess Brigid. Brigid's association with this festival is so strong that many Pagans regardless of their path or pantheon will honor Brigid during this celebration. The name Imbolc means "in the belly", and it is within the belly of the earth that life now stirs. For many northern areas it will be a while before the signs of spring appear above the lands of ice and snow, but slowly the earth is shifting and stretching in preparation of the spring to come.

Although Imbolc is a festival with very feminine energy and often celebrates the Feminine Divine as Maiden, we can also celebrate the Masculine Divine as the now growing new born Sun. The God is a young child still, but as the growing golden child, he trails light and warmth across the land.

Many urban Witches lack the agricultural connection of this festival, and the references of ewe's milk and lambing may be lost in translation, but the themes of fire and water associated with Imbolc can be inspirational to each Pagan regardless of location. The concept of personal purification and home blessings, or of increasing light and energy, is also a source of ritual inspiration.

In this sample ritual I have avoided dedicating the rite to Brigid not because I do not honor her, but because there are so many resources available for rites that center around Brigid. Instead, I wanted to offer an alternative ritual that focuses upon the increasing light and energy, both within the world around us and within ourselves. Hopefully, this kind of alternative will inspire your own unique rituals that work with your own personal associations and understanding of the seasonal celebrations.

HP/S: Sweep and clear

Be gone from here
Shift darkness from heart and mind
Bless this space
A sacred place
A time outside of time.
HPS: I draw this circle about us,
In the presence of the elements and Divine spirit
That we may be aided by the Lord and Lady and be blessed
by our work this night
The boundary of our circle lies below our feet,
Above our heads
Around our bodies
That we may work within a sphere of protection and love
And protection and love may work within us
The circle is charged and cast, so mote it be.
All: So mote it be.
NQ: Powers of North and Earth
Of fertile field and woodland shrine
Gift us with strength and fertility
For the duration of this rite
Hail and welcome!
All: Hail and welcome!
EQ: Powers of East and Air
Of wild storms and winds benign
Gift us with intellect and creativity
For the duration of this rite
Hail and welcome!
All: Hail and welcome!
SQ: Powers of South and Fire
Of burning flame that lights the night
Gift us with passion and virility
For the duration of this rite
Hail and welcome!
All: Hail and welcome!

WQ: Powers of West and Water
Of oceans deep and tears of mine
Gift us with love and empathy
For the duration of this rite
Hail and welcome!
All: Hail and welcome!
HPS: Beloved Lady, our Feminine Divine
We ask you here at this time outside of time
To a place of trust and love between
All that is and is yet unseen
Pause a while with us during this rite
Bless us with your wisdom and watchful sight
Let your compassion, experience and grace
Work through this Priestess in your place
Hail and welcome!
All: Hail and welcome!
HP: Beloved Lord, our Masculine Divine
We ask you here at this time outside of time
To a place of trust and love between
All that is and is yet unseen
Pause a while with us during this rite
Bless us with your wisdom and watchful sight
May the heat and the hunter now coarse through
This humble Priest that speaks for you
Hail and welcome!
All: Hail and welcome!
HPS: Welcome to the festival of light
Where springtime lies within our sight
Earth softens and milk flows
Babies are born, seeds are sown
Soon the thaws will flood the streams
And winter becomes the land of dreams
The Crone returns to the land of snow
And all around us light now grows

Hold high your flame, shine your light
Chase back the shadows and shrinking night
Prepare the path for spring to come
And rejoice now in the growing sun!

This is an appropriate time for each participant to light candles for a group meditation, or burn purification herbs in the cauldron.

HP: Deep in the belly of the earth life now stirs
Awakening within and shaking free of ice and snow
The Goddess carries the child of promise within her arms
Trailing light and warmth wherever he goes
Slowly the world awakens from its slumber
Pushing shadows back from long cold night
All around
Life abounds
Reaching out towards the growing light.

HPS: At this point in the Wheel of the Year, we feel our energy shake off the slumber of winter and rise like the dawn. As the light increases, so does our energy. This is an appropriate time to honor our Gods and ourselves by planning projects for the year ahead, activities of personal and spiritual growth, projects to develop our personal talents, ideas for developing new skills, dreams to chase, inspiration for individual and group endeavors. May all those who wish to, write down their thoughts, and burn them within the cauldron. Let the smoke rise to the skies and carry your intention out into the universe.

HP: Now we will all participate in waking the earth with drumming, dance and song. Raise your voices, raise your energy, and focus upon the waking earth and a safe rebirth!

All participants get up and get moving, stamping feet, clapping, dancing, drumming and chanting. Unless the group has a specific goal for the energy raised, then the focus should be upon the earth and any healing that the earth requires in your area.

Suggested chant:
Raise our voices
Stamp our feet
Awaken now the earth that sleeps.
HP: The cycle of the year promises bounty and sustenance even whilst we shiver still from winter's touch. May we share in this bounty to remind ourselves of the blessings of the Earth.
From the sun to the corn
From the corn to the flour
From the flour to the bread
May we be blessed by this bounty
May we never hunger
We consecrate this bread in the name of the Lord and Lady
Eat and be merry
HPS: From the rain to the vine
From the vine to the fruit
From the fruit to the wine
May we be blessed by this bounty
May we never thirst
We consecrate this wine in the name of the Lord and Lady
Drink and be merry.

Bread and wine are shared by all participants, providing an opportunity to ground and center after the energy raising and release.

HPS: Beloved Lady; Mother, Wisewoman and Daughter,
We thank you for your presence in this rite,
May you always reside in our hearts and minds,
As we bid you farewell this night
We extinguish this flame knowing it is but a symbol of you

Hail and farewell!

All: Hail and farewell!

HP: Beloved Lord; Father, Sage and Son,

We thank you for your presence in this rite,

May you always reside in our hearts and minds,

As we bid you farewell this night

We extinguish this flame knowing it is but a symbol of you

Hail and farewell!

All: Hail and farewell!

NQ: Powers of North and Earth

Of fertile field and woodland shrine

We thank you for your presence here

In this blessed rite

Go if you wish, stay if you will

Hail and farewell!

All: Hail and farewell!

EQ: Powers of East and Air

Of wild storms and winds benign

We thank you for your presence here

In this blessed rite

Go if you wish, stay if you will

Hail and Farewell!

All: Hail and farewell!

SQ: Powers of South and Fire

Of burning flame that lights the night

We thank you for your presence here

In this blessed rite

Go if you wish, stay if you will

Hail and farewell!

All: Hail and farewell!

WQ: Powers of West and Water

Of oceans deep and tears of mine

We thank you for your presence here

In this blessed rite

Go if you wish, stay if you will
Hail and farewell!

All: Hail and farewell!

HPS: Now our magic has been raised and released
We release the circle that contained it all
May the energy find its way to balance or purpose
And the site be at peace
Our rite has ended
So mote it be.

All: So mote it be

HP: We bless all those who have attended
And participated in this rite
May you carry the joy from this celebration
In your hearts for many a night
Our rite has ended. Merry meet, merry part and merry meet
  again!

All: Merry meet, merry part and merry meet again!

Ostara / Spring Equinox – 21st March

The Spring Equinox is a point of balance upon the Wheel of the Year. At this time light and darkness, day and night, are of approximately the same length, although light is gaining. It is the time when the Gods of light shake free of their alter egos, the Gods of darkness and shadow; and the time when the dying and rising Gods and Goddesses rise again from the underworld with new knowledge of life, death and rebirth. The grieving Earth Mothers celebrate the return of their loved ones, and the joy of reunion is visible in the earth's blessings of flora and fauna.

The rise of new life abounds in the fertile earth, and plants stretch forth towards the sun. Leaves adorn the trees, the earth is turned and seeds are sown for the coming harvest. This festival is all about rebirth, new life, new projects, hope and happiness.

> **HP/S:** Sweep and clear
> Be gone from here
> Shift winter from heart and mind
> Bless this space
> A sacred place
> A time outside of time.
> **HPS:** As the planets turn and circle one another
> In the universal dance of infinity
> I turn and circle this place of power
> And create a boundary of universal energy
> Within and around
> Magic abounds
> In the dance of eternal creation
> Universal I am
> Cyclical I am
> A tool of transformation
> I hold this space

A sacred place
A cauldron of manifestation
Now at last
The circle cast
By my will and invocation.
All: So mote it be!
NQ: Powers of North and Earth
Of fertile field and woodland shrine
Gift us with strength and fertility
For the duration of this rite
Hail and welcome!
All: Hail and welcome!
EQ: Powers of East and Air
Of wild storms and winds benign
Gift us with intellect and creativity
For the duration of this rite
Hail and welcome!
All: Hail and welcome!
SQ: Powers of South and Fire
Of burning flame that lights the night
Gift us with passion and virility
For the duration of this rite
Hail and welcome!
All: Hail and welcome!
WQ: Powers of West and Water
Of oceans deep and tears of mine
Gift us with love and empathy
For the duration of this rite
Hail and welcome!
All: Hail and welcome!
HPS: We all come from the Goddess
And to her we shall return
Like a drop of rain
Ever flowing to the ocean

We ask that you now join with us
Impart your wisdom and your grace
Passion and fertility now speak
Through the Priestess in your place
Hail to the Beloved Goddess!
All: Hail to the Beloved Goddess!
HP: We all come from the Green God
And to him we shall return
Within the woodland creatures
And the winter fires burn
We ask that you now join with us
Impart your life philosophy
The heat and the hunter rises up
Within the Priest that speaks for thee
Hail to the Beloved God!
All: Hail to the Beloved God!
HPS: Today we gather to bid farewell to the winter, and hail in the spring. We celebrate the turning of the wheel, and welcome the new season. We welcome home the dying and rising Gods, every Deity who returns from the Underworld with wisdom, knowledge and joy of rebirth. With their return our beloved Mother Earth blooms.

Every participant has the opportunity of placing a spring flower into a woven wreath in honor of the spring and the returning Gods. If you do not wish to use cut flowers, paper primulas can be made ahead of schedule to use as an alternative.

HP: Today we gather in balance, unity, and diversity, for we stand in a time of balance between light and dark, balance between feminine and masculine, balance between seasons. From this day on, the growing light chases back the shadows of winter and illuminates the earth. In response, our beloved Mother Earth blooms.

Every participant has the opportunity of lighting a candle to celebrate the growing light and to chase back the shadows of winter. It is common to light candles upon the altar, but glass jars with tealight candles inside are a lovely alternative for creating a circle of light. Candles may be lit from a long yellow God candle lit by the High Priest, passed deosil hand to hand, each participant lighting their own candle until the entire circle is lit and the God candle is returned to the altar.

HPS: Today we gather to plant the seeds of thought we have nurtured during the cold dark months, to bring our thoughts to light, and to grant them the blessings of our Gods. Please write down your goals or intentions that you wish to nurture, grow or harvest this year. Each intention will be wrapped around a seed and planted. As the seed grows, so will your intention, should that be for your highest good.

If your coven or group has its own land to use, intentions may be planted in the circle which will create a floral circle for future celebrations. If this is not an option, plant pots of dirt can be used on site and nurtured at home, or small bags of earth and a seed can be given to each participant to complete this ritual at home. If you do not wish to use ink, in consideration to your seed, then vegetable dyes or natural food coloring can be substituted. Do not wrap your seeds too tightly, as they must have room to grow, and water them well.

HP: Let us raise our voices and our energy in blessing of the new season and in celebration of the rising Gods. Dance, drum, sing and share your love!
All: This is the time
This is the hour
Here and now
We raise our power

Repeat this chant until the energy is at its peak. It is the duty of the

High Priestess and High Priest to harness the energy for release and signal the point of release to all the participants. Rapid drumming followed by three slow, distinct and loud drumbeats works well as a signal. You may also wish to incorporate your circle of light in the release by each participant dropping to the floor and blowing out their candles, letting the energy release with the smoke of the extinguished candles.

HPS: The energy is raised and released to fulfill its purpose within the world. Please take a moment to shake off any excess energy, to ground and to center.

HP: You are the tree. The leaf trembling in the breeze is but a part of you. The leaf secured by the branch is but a part of you. The branch growing from the trunk is but a part of you. The trunk rooted deep in the earth is but a part of you. The roots spreading through the earth are but a part of you. You are the tree, vibrant and alive, rooted and secure. Feel your deep connection to earth and sky. Feel your connection to the Divine all. Be calm, grounded, at peace.

HPS: Let us now share in the bounty of the Divine, for spring is the promise of harvest.

From the sun to the corn
From the corn to the flour
From the flour to the bread
May we be blessed by this bounty
May we never hunger
We consecrate this bread in the name of the Lord and Lady
Eat and be merry.

Each participant to share in the giving and receiving of bread.

HP: From the rain to the vine
From the vine to the fruit
From the fruit to the wine

May we be blessed by this bounty
May we never thirst
We consecrate this wine in the name of the Lord and Lady
Drink and be merry.

Each participant to share in the giving and receiving of wine.

HPS: Blessed be the gracious Goddess
Mother of all to whom we shall return
We thank you for blessing our gathering with your presence
In gratitude we say hail and farewell
All: Beloved Goddess, hail and farewell!
HP: Blessed be the Green God
Father of all to whom we shall return
We thank you for blessing our gathering with your presence
In gratitude we say hail and farewell.
All: Beloved God, hail and farewell!
WQ: Powers of West and Water
Of oceans deep and tears of mine
We thank you for your presence here
In this blessed rite
Go if you wish, stay if you will
Hail and farewell!
All: Hail and farewell!
SQ: Powers of South and Fire
Of burning flame that lights the night
We thank you for your presence here
In this blessed rite
Go if you wish, stay if you will
Hail and farewell!
All: Hail and farewell!
EQ: Powers of East and Air
Of wild storms and winds benign
We thank you for your presence here

In this blessed rite
Go if you wish, stay if you will
Hail and farewell!
All: Hail and farewell!
NQ: Powers of North and Earth
Of fertile field and woodland shrine
We thank you for your presence here
In this blessed rite
Go if you wish, stay if you will
Hail and farewell!
All: Hail and farewell!
HPS: I draw back the energy of the circle
And send it down to our Mother Earth
The circle is released from purpose to be reborn again
As I will it, so mote it be.
All: So mote it be!
HP: Let us carry this magic in our hearts,
As our rite ends and we now depart
Bid fond farewell as the day wanes
Merry met, merry part, merry we meet again
All: Merry met, merry part, merry we meet again!

Beltaine / May Day – 1st May

Beltaine, a fire festival, is a celebration of the time of light and a celebration of the union between God and Goddess. It is a fertility festival that honors all forms of fertility and creativity; the fertility of land, of nature, of animals, of humanity and of divinity. The union between the God and Goddess is celebrated as the King and Queen of May with song, dance and merriment. Fires are lit to honor the time of light, passion and abundance, and reflect the purification and transformation of the new life that abounds during the spring. The veil between the worlds is thin at Beltaine, as it is during the festival of Samhain, making it an ideal time for divinatory arts and connection with the realm of spirits. The Celtic year was divided into two seasons, summer and winter, and it is believed these were marked by Beltaine and Samhain, making Beltaine the beginning of the summer months, a season of planting, a season of plenty, a season of harvest.

HP/S: As I sweep, may this place be cleansed
From all debris of mind and heart
Chase away the negativity
Sweep and clear our path.
HPS: Here lies the boundary of my circle
Formed through matter and spirit
Only those with knowledge of the password are welcome here
In love and trust
In will and wisdom
By the power of the Divine that lies in me
I cast in strength and form in love
As I will it, so mote it be.
HP: So mote it be.

Participants enter the circle through the door cut by the High Priestess,

*either side of the door guarded by the High Priestess and High Priest.
Participants are anointed upon entrance.*

HP: I anoint thee in the name of the Lord and Lady.
Participant: Blessed be.
HPS: How do you enter this ritual?
Participant: In perfect love and perfect trust.

*Once all participants are welcomed into the circle, the circle is sealed
and the ritual progresses.*

NQ: Greetings and blessings to North and Earth
Mother of all and womb of manifestation
We welcome your strength and stability
In our circle of celebration
May you be at home in the sanctuary of our arms
Hail and welcome.
All: Hail and welcome!
EQ: Greetings and blessings to East and Air
Father of word and whispered wisdom
We welcome your thought and inspiration
In our circle of celebration
May you be at ease in the sanctuary of our minds
Hail and welcome.
All: Hail and welcome!
SQ: Greetings and blessings to South and Fire
Brother of destruction, creation and transformation
We welcome your passion and vitality
In our circle of celebration
May you be in comfort in the sanctuary of our spirit
Hail and welcome.
All: Hail and welcome!
WQ: Greetings and blessings to West and Water
Sister of life and emotional tides

We welcome your purity and understanding
In our circle of celebration
May you be at peace in the sanctuary of our hearts
Hail and welcome.
All: Hail and welcome!
HP: Listen now to the words of your Goddess as she speaks through this Priestess in her place.
HPS: I am the time outside of time,
And the cycle that time revolves around
I am the spark of life found in all things
Both within this reality and without
I am the laughter of children found in bleak winter cold
I am the tears of lovers drying in the summer sun
I am the desire of youth burning within the old
I am the honest relief found when death comes
I reside in your hopes and fears
And spiral through the lands of your dreams
I am the unforgiving sense of familiarity
When life is no longer as it seems
I am the challenge of every new born life
I am the hunger that still seeks when all are fed
I am the joy discovered after hardness and strife
I am the cold light of truth when lies have been shed.
I cannot be called nor coaxed,
Summoned nor stirred,
Begged nor bound,
For I am a part of all things at all times in many ways
I can flow through or form within,
Pass by or pause,
Gather in and gift out,
And speak through you, to you, in honor of the Old Ways.
All: Hail beloved Goddess!
HPS: Listen now to the words of your God as he speaks through this Priest in his place.

HP: Hear my words upon the winds of winter
And subtle summer breeze
Hear my words of truth when you turn towards me
I am the times of change, the cycle of sun
The blessings of bounty and battles won
I am the voice of dissent, of counsel and reason
The hardworking hand of hurt and healing
I am dark and light, day and night,
Harvest and sacrifice
I am cold death and blessed rebirth
The Lord of Shadows and the Green Man of earth
I am the rebelliousness of youth
The wisdom of old age
I am Squire, Knight, Priest and Sage
Seek and you shall find me
For I am within all things, at all times, in many ways
From times passed to future days
I am within each life born
Within each death transformed
Within the very reflection of your gaze
Raise your eyes
For I reside
Within your soul
Call to me and I shall come home
For I am within all things, at all times, in many ways.
All: Hail beloved God!
All the Quarters in unison:
Great God, Beloved Goddess
Tonight you grace us with your presence
You are the embodiment of the Divine
A Divinity that touches the lives of each person here
From every heart within this circle
We offer you our love
Blessed be.

All: Blessed be

HPS: Blessed be the Queen of May

The tempting Goddess full of desire

Blessed be the Green God of fertility

The hunter and hunted, lighting sacred fires.

HP: Life-giving God and Goddess

Together as one, united as one

Bringing fertility to the lands

A sacred union of Earth and Sun.

All: Blessed be the union!

HPS: Light the fires!

Feel the heat!

Raise your voices!

Stamp your feet!

You are the chase, you are the kiss!

You are the life that gives!

Feel the love, feel the desire!

Chase your passion between the fires!

A fire maze or twin fires are lit for participants to run around and in between. If your sacred space does not allow for such fires, candles within cauldrons or even red and gold colored streamers can be substituted. Many groups will enact a form of "kiss chase" with participants chased between the fires and kissed, but please be aware of the sexual overtones of this Beltaine celebration and consider its appropriateness for your ritual participants. Love and sex are positive aspects of Pagan practice, but laughter and fun are also important so keep it lighthearted and in good spirits. When every participant has been through the flames, the High Priest and Priestess must harness any raised energy for release and signal the participants to ground and center.

HPS: Be seated, and be still your racing hearts. Join with us in contemplation and meditation. Close your eyes and listen.

HP: The heartbeat

Drumbeat
The pulse of Earth quickens
The rivers rushing
The oceans heaving
The land bedecked in finery
Calling forth the touch of rain, of sun
Every flower reaching out for the sun's caress
Turning their faces towards the kiss of light
Every leaf trembling at the whispers of the wind
Fresh green grass wet with dew
The forests filled with the sounds of life
Every creature calling out for a mate
The earth herself awake
Restless
Seeking
Searching
Stretching
Reaching out for her lover
Responding to the touch of light
Chasing back the shadows of winter
And falling in love
Once again
The earth in throes of ecstasy
A sacred union laid bare
For all to see
The beloved earth replies
To a love that lights the whole sky.

HPS: And so we feel the passion of the Gods, the fertility of our world and the joy of sacred union. Through fire we are cleansed and pure, free in passion and joy. Through earth we give and receive, free in love and fertility. May we carry this passion and joy into all the aspects of our life we wish to grow and nurture.

HP: Open your eyes and revel in all your senses. Let us join together to share in the blessings of the Mother Goddess and her consort the Green God.

HP: As the athame is to the male.

HPS: So the chalice is to the female.

Both: For what one lacks, the other may give
There is no greater power in the universe than that of love
Blessed be this union.

All: Blessed be!

HPS: From the sun to the corn
From the corn to the flour
From the flour to the bread
May we be blessed by this bounty
May we never hunger
We consecrate this bread in the name of the Lord and Lady
Eat and be merry.

Each participant to share in the giving and receiving of bread.

HP: From the rain to the flowers
From the flowers to the bees
From the bees to the honey
From the honey to the mead
May we be blessed by this bounty
May we never thirst
We consecrate this mead in the name of the Lord and Lady
Drink and be merry.

Each participant to share in the giving and receiving of mead.

HPS: Blessed be the gracious Goddess
Mother of all to whom we shall return
We thank you for blessing our gathering with your presence
In gratitude we say hail and farewell.

All: Hail and farewell!

HP: Blessed be the Green God
Father of all to whom we shall return
We thank you for blessing our gathering with your presence
In gratitude we say hail and farewell.
All: Hail and farewell!
WQ: Farewell blessings to West and Water
Sister of life and emotional tides
We thank your purity and understanding
In our circle of celebration
Go if you wish, stay if you will
Hail and farewell.
All: Hail and farewell!
SQ: Farewell blessings to South and Fire
Brother of destruction, creation and transformation
We thank your passion and vitality
In our circle of celebration
Go if you wish, stay if you will
Hail and farewell.
All: Hail and farewell!
EQ: Farewell blessings to East and Air
Father of word and whispered wisdom
We thank your thought and inspiration
In our circle of celebration
Go if you wish, stay if you will
Hail and farewell.
All: Hail and farewell!
NQ: Farewell blessings to North and Earth
Mother of all and womb of manifestation
We thank your strength and stability
In our circle of celebration
Go if you wish, stay if you will
Hail and farewell.
All: Hail and farewell!
HPS: Blessed circle cast around

I release thee unto the ground
Unto the air to scatter free
Unto the storms, unto the sea
Go find your home within the All
As circle is released, our boundary falls
So mote it be.
All: So mote it be!
HP: We bless all those who have attended
And participated in this rite
May you carry the joy from this celebration
In your hearts for many a night
Merry meet, merry part, merry meet again!
All: Merry meet, merry part, merry meet again!

Litha / Summer Solstice – 21st June

Summer Solstice, the opposite and equal of Winter Solstice, is also known as Litha. This festival marks the highest point of light within the Wheel of the Year, the longest day and the shortest night. As with all peaks of power, the highest point of the light's strength is also the tipping point into a time of darkness and shadow. From this point on, light starts to wane and the darkness grows a little each day, which means the celebration of summer is also the first steps towards winter.

As with many festivals, there are several themes for Summer Solstice celebrations. Honoring the strength and power of the God of Light, celebrating the marriage of the God and Goddess, blessing the Goddess heavy with pregnancy, and enacting the battle between light and dark are all common practices for Summer Solstice. The battle between the Holly King and the Oak King, so often presented during Winter Solstice celebrations, is the theme for the ritual below.

HPS: My hand upon the besom guides away all unwanted, unneeded energies. My hand upon the besom clears and cleanses this space. By my hand, by my will, I sweep and cleanse ready for the blessings of the Divine.
HP: I conjure thee
Circle of power
That you may be a boundary between the worlds
That you may be a place between times
That you may protect those within its walls
That you may contain the power raised within
I bless and consecrate thee in the essence of the elements
I bless and consecrate thee in the names of the Lord and Lady.
Be formed now in strength and love
So mote it be.

All: So mote it be!

NQ: Hail to the Gnomes of Earth
Of flesh and bone, mud and mountain
Bring the gift of a solid foundation
To the magic woven within this rite
Welcome to our circle.

All: Hail and welcome!

EQ: Hail to the Sylphs of Air
Of breath and thought, breeze and gale
Bring the gift of inspiration and knowledge
To the magic woven within this rite
Welcome to our circle.

All: Hail and welcome!

SQ: Hail to the Salamanders of Fire
Of heart and blood, light and flame
Bring the gift of a focused Will
To the magic woven within this rite
Welcome to our circle.

All: Hail and welcome!

WQ: Hail to the Undines of Water
Of hormonal tides, sea and stream
Bring the gift of simple truth
To the magic woven within this rite
Welcome to our circle.

All: Hail and welcome!

HPS: Beloved Lady, our Feminine Divine
We ask you here at this time outside of time
To a place of trust and love between
All that is and is yet unseen
Pause a while with us during this rite
Bless us with your wisdom and watchful sight
Let your compassion, experience and grace
Work through this Priestess in your place
Hail and welcome!

All: Hail and welcome!

HP: Beloved Lord, our Masculine Divine
We ask you here at this time outside of time
To a place of trust and love between
All that is and is yet unseen
Pause a while with us during this rite
Bless us with your wisdom and watchful sight
May the heat and the hunter now coarse through
This humble Priest that speaks for you
Hail and welcome!

All: Hail and welcome!

HPS: We gather today to celebrate the Summer Solstice, the height of the sun's power and the tipping point of the wheel. Today the God as Oak King stands strong and tall, prepared to face the challenge of Lord Holly, who seeks to take the crown.

Should you wish to include a physical re-enactment of the Battle between Holly and Oak, this is an opportune time for two participants to represent the Holly King and the Oak King in duel. Dress participants appropriately so that the battle is clear to all spectators. It is advisable to choreograph the battle and practice this ahead of schedule.

HP: The Holly and the Oak
When they are both full grown
The Oak King fights the Holly King
Upon Midwinter's morn.

HPS: The Oak King slays the Holly King
And reigns for half a year
The Holly King rises again
When winter's breath draws near.

HP: The Holly King lays challenge
Upon Midsummer's day
Holly King slays Oak King

And bears the crown away.

HPS: When the sun comes round again
At waxing of the year
The Oak King rises up once more
For his time of reign draws near.

HP: And so at the height of light, the shadows draw close and Holly strikes a mortal blow. As the Oak Kings lays wounded, Holly bears the crown away to rule the darkening half of the year. The Oak is king no more, his power fading as the light wanes, but still he offers what remains of his power and sovereignty to the people of all the lands. His life blood feeds the fields, and at the harvest he scatters the last of his life into the crops that sustain us over the winter months. This future act of sacrifice is the end of Oak's life above, but the beginning of his journey below. Oak will be our dying and rising God, emerging strong and triumphant from his rest and rebirth to challenge the Holly King once more and take his place as King of the Waxing Sun.

High Priestess lights a gold candle in honor of the Oak King.

HPS: We light a candle for Lord Oak, its trembling flame a reminder of his power and sovereignty in the growing darkness. The Oak King is defeated, long live the Oak King!
All: The Oak King is defeated, long live the Oak King!

The High Priest lights a gold candle in honor of the Holly King.

HP: All hail the Holly King! Ruler of the all the lands!
All: All hail the Holly King! Ruler of the all the lands!
HP: It is the cycle of life and death and rebirth that is revealed on the brightest of days as well as the darkest of days. As we celebrate the time of growth, energy and abundance, we are also shown the stories of sacrifice, introspection and loss.

HPS: As people of the land, we understand this duality within the world around us and within our own inner landscape. Just as the Oak King and Holly King are one and the same, so do we bear our own light and shadows, our own wax and wane. Please light your candles to illuminate the circle in honor of the longest day, the height of light, and the light within us all.

All participants to light a candle from the Oak King candle. When the circle is lit, the Oak King and Holly King may wish to lead a chant to raise energy for the Oak King in his new role as dying and rising God. The chant can be ended and released with the extinguishing of the candles.

Suggested chant:
Around me now the power grows
As above so below
Within me now the power flows
As above so below.
HP: As the athame is to the male.
HPS: So the chalice is to the female.
HP: For what one lacks, the other may give.
HPS: There is no greater power in the universe than that of love.
Both: Blessed be the union.
All: Blessed be!
HP: From the sun to the corn
From the corn to the flour
From the flour to the bread
May we be blessed by this bounty
May we never hunger
We consecrate this bread in the name of the Lord and Lady
Eat and be merry.

Each participant to share in the giving and receiving of bread.

> **HPS:** From the rain to the vine
> From the vine to the fruit
> From the fruit to the wine
> May we be blessed by this bounty
> May we never thirst
> We consecrate this wine in the name of the Lord and Lady.
> Drink and be merry.

Each participant to share in the giving and receiving of wine.

> **HP:** Blessed God, Holly and Oak, Lord of Light
> We thank you for your presence this night
> Go if you must, stay if you will
> With gratitude we say hail and farewell.
> **All:** Hail and farewell!
> **HPS:** Blessed Goddess, beloved Divine,
> We thank you for your presence this night
> Go if you must, stay if you will
> With gratitude we say hail and farewell.
> **All:** Hail and farewell!
> **WQ:** Farewell to the Undines of Water
> Of hormonal tides, sea and stream
> Thank you for your gifts woven within this rite
> Go if you wish, stay if you will
> Hail and farewell.
> **All:** Hail and farewell!
> **SQ:** Farewell to the Salamanders of Fire
> Of heart and blood, light and flame
> Thank you for your gifts woven within this rite
> Go if you wish, stay if you will
> Hail and farewell.
> **All:** Hail and farewell!

EQ: Farewell to the Sylphs of Air
Of breath and thought, breeze and gale
Thank you for your gifts woven within this rite
Go if you wish, stay if you will
Hail and farewell.
All: Hail and farewell!
NQ: Farewell to the Gnomes of Earth
Of flesh and bone, mud and mountain
Thank you for your gifts woven within this rite
Go if you wish, stay if you will
Hail and farewell.
All: Hail and farewell!
HP: This circle has served well
Time has come to say farewell
I release the energy of its bond
And return it all to where it belongs
As above
So below.
All: So mote it be!
HPS: We bless all those who have attended
And participated in this rite
May you carry the joy from this celebration
In your hearts for many a night
Merry meet, merry part, merry meet again!
All: Merry meet, merry part, merry meet again!

Lughnasadh / Lammas – 1st August

Lammas is the first of the three harvest festivals, a celebration of the bounty provided by Mother Earth. Hay and corn are cut, the first breads are baked with new flour, food and the bounty of nature are honored.

The name Lughnasadh also signifies the celebration of the Celtic God Lugh, and his many skills are honored in games and competitions. In many traditions this first harvest festival is also a celebration of sacrifice, when the God of Light – so recently wounded and defeated by the God of Darkness at the Summer Solstice – gives the last of his energy over to the bounty of the earth and scatters his remaining strength into the fields to bless the harvest. This sacrifice reminds us that a time of personal harvest is also a time of endings, a time of letting go.

HPS: My hand upon the besom guides away all unwanted, unneeded energies. My hand upon the besom clears and cleanses this space. By my hand, by my will, I sweep and cleanse ready for the blessings of the Divine.

HP: I cast a circle of power above and below, inside and outside, around and about me
Strengthened by Earth
Formed by Air
Charged by Fire
Cleansed by Water
Consecrated by Spirit
As above, 'tis so below
This circle is cast
So mote it be.

All: So mote it be!

NQ: I call upon the blessings and energy of North and Earth! Blessings manifest in the fruits of the harvest, in the crops and corn, in the giving earth, and in the soil we stand upon. Share with us the mystery of bounty, of growth and diversity. Gift us with your qualities. Be with us now during this blessed rite, be with us now as we celebrate the Divine. Hail and welcome!

All: Hail and welcome!

EQ: I call upon the blessings and energy of East and Air! Blessings manifest within the sharing of knowledge, in the scattering of seed, in the whispering corn fields, and in the gentle breeze. Share with us the mystery of inspiration, of connection and communication. Gift us with your qualities. Be with us now during this blessed rite, be with us now as we celebrate the Divine. Hail and welcome!

All: Hail and welcome!

SQ: I call upon the blessings and energy of South and Fire! Blessings manifest in the sun ripened earth, in the warmth of skin, in the abundant sun, and in the fire within. Share with us the mystery of wax and wane, of shadow and flame. Gift us with your qualities. Be with us now during this blessed rite, be with us now as we celebrate the Divine. Hail and welcome!

All: Hail and welcome!

WQ: I call upon the blessings and energy of West and Water! Blessings manifest in the taste of sweet fruits, in the thirst slaked, in the rain-washed fields, and in the bountiful lakes. Share with us the mystery of rise and subside, of emotional tides. Gift us with your qualities. Be with us now during this blessed rite, be with us now as we celebrate the Divine. Hail and welcome!

All: Hail and welcome!

HPS: Beloved Lady, our Feminine Divine
We ask you here at this time outside of time
To a place of trust and love between
All that is and is yet unseen

Pause a while with us during this rite
Bless us with your wisdom and watchful sight
Let your compassion, experience and grace
Work through this Priestess in your place
Hail and welcome!

All: Hail and welcome!

HP: Beloved Lord, our Masculine Divine
We ask you here at this time outside of time
To a place of trust and love between
All that is and is yet unseen
Pause a while with us during this rite
Bless us with your wisdom and watchful sight
May the heat and the hunter now coarse through
This humble Priest that speaks for you
Hail and welcome!

All: Hail and welcome!

HPS: We gather today to celebrate the bounty of the Divine, manifest within as a personal harvest and manifest without as the first harvest festival. We honor the dying and rising Gods who start their journey into the underworld of shadows, the sacrifice they make for the cycle of our seasons, and the knowledge they will bring forth when they rise again.

HP: We face our own harvests, based upon the seeds we have sown this year. We acknowledge the work we have put into our dreams and achievements, the weeding out of that which no longer serves us, and the blessing of our own bounty.

HPS: Even as we gather in our harvest, we are reminded of the seeds we plant for the future. Take these seeds as a reminder of the continual spiritual cycle of planting, growing, tending, harvesting, resting, and replenishing.

Each participant is given a small bag of seeds or ears of corn as a blessing of the first harvest and a reminder of the seasonal cycle. Seeds may be passed hand to hand deosil around the circle so that each partic-

ipant both gives and receives.

All: May the rains sweep gentle across your fields
May the sun warm the land
May every good seed you have planted bear fruit
And late summer find you standing in fields of plenty.
HPS: The blooming Goddess, who already carries the light of the new God within her, must now say farewell to her consort as he prepares for his journey to the Underworld. This reminds us that even a time of light is touched by shadow, and a time of plenty is touched by loss.
HP: The beloved God of Light, wounded by his alter ego the Lord of Shadow, now relinquishes his rule of the world and becomes the God of Sacrifice. He scatters the last of his energy into the first harvest, so that we may be blessed by his touch. Let us share in the journey of the Divine by raising and releasing energy into the harvest, both physical and spiritual.
HPS: Join hands and raise your voices in honor of the God and Goddess!

All participants link hands and dance around the circle. Many paths will dance widdershins to represent the God's descent. It is the duty of the High Priest and Priestess to manage the raising of energy and signal the release of energy to the participants.

All: Dance, dance, wherever ye may be!
When you dance with the Lord, he will dance with thee
Turn, turn, a circle then ye form!
And the Lord of the Dance is the Lord of the Corn
Down, down, into the earth he'll go!
Giving life to the grain that in the spring we'll sow
He rules the Shadow Lands 'til Yule
When his Sun is reborn and his life renewed!
HPS: Let us now share in the bounty of this harvest, and

enjoy all the blessings of physical and spiritual harvests. We shall bless and consecrate the bread and wine in honor of the God and Goddess, and then share out this simple feast. If you wish to also share your spiritual harvest this year, you may verbalize your blessings as we give and receive this bounty.

HP: From the sun to the corn

From the corn to the flour

From the flour to the bread

May we be blessed by this bounty

May we never hunger

We consecrate this bread in the name of the Lord and Lady

Eat and be merry.

Each participant to share in the giving and receiving of bread. If a participant wishes to share their spiritual harvest, this is an appropriate time to count blessings.

HPS: From the rain to the vine

From the vine to the fruit

From the fruit to the wine

May we be blessed by this bounty

May we never thirst

We consecrate this wine in the name of the Lord and Lady

Drink and be merry.

Each participant to share in the giving and receiving of wine.

HP: Blessed God of dark and light,

We thank you for your presence this night

Go if you must, stay if you will

With gratitude we say hail and farewell.

All: Hail and farewell.

HPS: Blessed Goddess, Mother Divine,

We thank you for your presence this night

Go if you must, stay if you will
With gratitude we say hail and farewell.
All: Hail and farewell.
WQ: Powers of West and Water
Of oceans deep, tears and tides
We thank you for your presence here in this blessed rite
Go if you wish, stay if you will
Hail and farewell.
All: Hail and farewell.
SQ: Powers of South and Fire
Of burning flame and gentle sunlight
We thank you for your presence here in this blessed rite
Go if you wish, stay if you will
Hail and farewell.
All: Hail and farewell.
EQ: Powers of East and Air
Of whispered thought and winds benign
We thank you for your presence here in this blessed rite
Go if you wish, stay if you will
Hail and farewell.
All: Hail and farewell.
NQ: Powers of North and Earth
Of fertile field and harvest time
We thank you for your presence here in this blessed rite
Go if you wish, stay if you will
Hail and farewell.
All: Hail and farewell.
HP: Blessed circle cast around
I release thee unto the ground
Unto the air to scatter free
Unto the storms, unto the sea
Go find your home within the All
As circle is released, our boundary falls
So mote it be.

All: So mote it be!

HPS: Blessings to us all, each one of us a part of the Divine we honored during this rite. May we carry the joy of this celebration in our hearts for many a night. Merry meet, merry part, and merry meet again.

All: Merry meet, merry part, and merry meet again!

Mabon / Autumn Equinox – 21st September

The Autumn Equinox marks a point of balance upon the Wheel of the Year, the opposite and equal of the Spring Equinox. At this point both light and dark, day and night, are of approximately equal length, but darkness is slowly gaining. The doors to the underworld open in preparation of the journey of the dying and rising Gods to travel below into the tomb and womb of the Great Mother, where they will become the Lords and Ladies of Darkness and Shadow. During the winter months they will learn the mysteries of life, death and rebirth, face their own shadow selves, gain knowledge of the deeper mysteries, and eventually be reborn again at spring.

Their descent into the underworld leaves all the Earth Mothers grieving, and sparks the cycle of autumn and winter. The rebirth of the dying and rising Gods will bring about the blessings and joy of spring and summer. This festival is sometimes called Mabon, after the young Welsh God stolen from his mother Modron just days after his birth and hidden until the his rebirth at the Winter Solstice.

The Autumn Equinox is the second harvest festival, and often revolves around the harvest and preservation of fruits. As a harvest festival this is a time of thanksgiving and a celebration of the bounty of nature, and as the tipping point when darkness takes a hold it is also a time of personal reflection and introspection.

> **HP/S:** As I wield a broom of old
> I do more than sweep the floor
> I chase away the negativity
> And push it out the door
> Begone!
> Begone!

There is work to be done.

HPS: I cast about this sacred space a circle of power

By the energy and elements of all that be

By sand, and sky, and sun, and sea

By Divine spirit external and within me

Above me, below me, around me

The boundary of my circle is cast

So mote it be.

All: So mote it be!

NQ: I call upon the power of Earth to bring strength to this rite.

EQ: I call upon the power of Air to bring clarity to this rite.

SQ: I call upon the power of Fire to bring focus to this rite.

WQ: I call upon the power of Water to bring wisdom to this rite.

All Quarters: We call to thee! We welcome thee! Blessed be!

All: We call to thee! We welcome thee! Blessed be!

HPS: Beloved Lady, our Feminine Divine

We ask you here at this time outside of time

To a place of trust and love between

All that is and is yet unseen

Pause a while with us during this rite

Bless us with your wisdom and watchful sight

Let your compassion, experience and grace

Work through this Priestess in your place

Hail and welcome.

All: Hail and welcome.

HP: Beloved Lord, our Masculine Divine

We ask you here at this time outside of time

To a place of trust and love between

All that is and is yet unseen

Pause a while with us during this rite

Bless us with your wisdom and watchful sight

May the heat and the hunter now coarse through

This humble Priest who speaks for you
Hail and welcome.
All: Hail and welcome.
HPS: Blessings of bright Mabon
Of graceful autumn presence
Blessings of balance
Of silver moon and golden sun
Blessings of bounty
Of seeds sown and harvest grown
Blessings of knowledge found
Between summer's kiss and winter's touch.
HP: As the circle turns and darkness reigns
Know all that falls shall rise again
For darkness, there is light
For sorrow, there is joy
For grief, there is love
For despair, there is hope
For loss, there is gain
Without one, the other is without meaning
The harvest of Mabon lies in more than home and hearth
Mabon is a harvest of the mind and heart
May the harvest be blessed and bountiful.
HPS: Tonight we will share the bounty of the second harvest, and share our stories of gratitude, personal harvest and personal sacrifice. As we bless this bounty of our God and Goddess and are in return blessed by their bounty, consider the seeds you have sown this year, the harvest you have reaped, the sacrifices you have made, and the seeds you wish to plant for the future.
HP: Goddess Divine
Within our hearts and minds
We thank you for the blessings bestowed upon us
With gratitude and joy
We offer this simple appreciation:

From the rain to the vine
From the vine to the fruit
From the fruit to the wine
May we be blessed by this bounty
May we never thirst
We consecrate this wine in the name of the Goddess Divine
Let us drink and be merry
HP: God Divine
Within our hearts and minds
We thank you for the blessings bestowed upon us
With gratitude and joy
We offer this simple appreciation:
From the sun to the corn
From the corn to the flour
From the flour to the bread
May we be blessed by this bounty
May we never hunger
We consecrate this bread in the name of the God Divine
Let us eat and be merry.

As the bread and wine are passed around the circle, each participant should state a simple gratitude for some aspect of their personal harvest. This is a thanksgiving that does not transfer ownership of personal blessings into the realm of Divinity, but accepts that we are each a part of the Divine, a part of the cycle of life, and respects the interconnectedness of all life. One may easily raise personal achievements without shame or guilt, for personal success is as worthy of celebration as the gifts and bounty of the universe. One cannot separate gratitude of the garden's bounty from the gardener that tends the plants.

HP: As darkness takes a hold, we must all prepare for our journeys inwards, just as the Gods prepare for their descent into the underworld. Take this time to consider the time after harvest, when the fields lay bare, when nature rests, when the breath of winter whispers to us. The increasing darkness encourages us to conserve our energy, to rest, to prepare and to plan for the future. It is a time of introspection and self-awareness.

HPS: Upon the altar is a mirror, paper and a cauldron. Each person should take the time to reflect upon themselves, consider their own inner journey, and write a few words of gratitude for their recent personal harvest or a prayer to the Divine for their future journey and cast it into the cauldron.

Each participant should take the time to visit the altar and place their words of gratitude or personal prayers into the cauldron that represents both the womb and the tomb of the Goddess. When every participant has completed this act, a chant to raise energy over the cauldron should be undertaken by all before the contents are set ablaze, the energy of the chant released with the fire and smoke.

Suggested chant (All):
Around me now the power grows
As above so below
Within me now the power flows
As above so below

HPS: May our words and thoughts soar high over hill and valley, land and sea. May our gratitude for the bounty bestowed upon us ripple through the world. Beloved Divine, we honor thee.

All: So mote it be

HP: Blessed God, we thank you for your presence
Go if you must, stay if you will
With gratitude we say hail and farewell.

All: Hail and farewell.

HPS: Blessed Goddess, we thank you for your presence
Go if you must, stay if you will
With gratitude we say hail and farewell.

All: Hail and farewell.

NQ: With earth we learned a new way.

EQ: With the wind we sang in a new day.

SQ: With the fire we burned to survive.

WQ: With water we respected our lives.

All Quarters: Blessed be to the elements of our world, we thank you for your presence in our lives. Hail and farewell.

All: Hail and farewell.

HPS: This circle has served well

Time has come to say farewell

I release the energy of its bond

And return it all to where it belongs

As above

So below

Circle open, never broken

So mote it be.

All: So mote it be.

HP: Blessings to us all, each one of us a part of the Divine we honored during this rite. May we carry the joy of this celebration in our hearts for many a night. Merry meet, merry part, and merry meet again.

All: Merry meet, merry part, merry meet again!

Ritual Correspondences

There is a wonderful array of resources available for spell and ritual correspondences / associations by many Pagan authors, so I have only provided a limited overview within this book. Please feel free to use these correspondences to assist you in designing your rituals and celebrations, or use them as a springboard for researching alternative correspondences. I would always recommend that you take the time to develop your own correspondence charts, since there are often regional variations and different associations within different practices. Find what works for you, discover which associations have the strongest impact or greatest resonance to you, and create your own correspondence charts for easy reference.

Days of the Week

Monday

Influences: Children; Clairvoyance; Dreams; Family; Femininity; Fertility; Healing; Home; Intuition; Mothers; Protection; Psychic Abilities; Water Magic; Women's Mysteries

Deities: Artemis; Diana; Isis; Luna; Mani; Selene; Thoth

Archangel: Gabriel

Planet: Moon

Element: Water

Colors: Silver; White; Grey

Herbs/Incense: Comfrey; Moonwort; Myrtle; Violet; Willow; Wintergreen; Wormwood

Trees: Alder; Eucalyptus; Willow

Crystals: Moonstone; Mother of Pearl; Opal; Pearl; Selenite

Metal: Silver

Tuesday

Influences: Armed Forces; Change; Courage; Health/Vitality;

Independence; Initiative; Lust; Overcoming the Odds; Protection; Resisting Injustice

Deities: Ares; Bellona; Mars; The Morrighan; Tiu; Tyr

Archangel: Samael

Planet: Mars

Element: Fire

Colors: Red; Orange

Herbs/Incense: Basil; Dragon's Blood; Patchouli

Trees: Cypress; Holly; Pine

Crystals: Bloodstone; Garnet; Jasper; Ruby

Metal: Iron; Steel

Wednesday

Influences: Business Negotiations; Communication; Medicine/ Surgery; Money Matters; Repelling Negativity; Study/Exams; Technology

Deities: Athena; Heimdall; Hermes; Iris; Mercury; Odin

Archangel: Raphael

Planet: Mercury

Element: Air

Colors: Grey; Violet; Yellow

Herbs/Incense: Jasmine; Lavender

Trees: Ash; Hazel; Silver Birch

Crystals: Agate; Citrine; Jasper; Malachite; Onyx

Metal: Aluminum; Mercury

Thursday

Influences: Authority; Careers; Fidelity; Honor; Increase; Justice; Law; Leadership; Loyalty; Marriage; Partnerships; Travel

Deities: Jupiter; Thor; Zeus

Archangel: Sachiel

Planet: Jupiter

Element: Air

Colors: Blue; Indigo; Purple

Herbs/Incense: Cinnamon; Clove; Nutmeg; Sage
Trees: Beech; Oak; Redwood
Crystals: Azurite; Lapis Lazuli; Sodalite; Turquoise
Metal: Tin

Friday
Influences: Arts; Beauty; Crafts; Environmental Matters; Fertility; Fidelity; Friendship; Love; Marriage; Peace; Relationships; Sexuality; Women's Health
Deities: Aphrodite; Freyja; Frigg; Inanna; Juno; Venus
Archangel: Anael
Planet: Venus
Element: Earth
Colors: Green; Pink
Herbs/Incense: Lime; Saffron; Sandalwood; Thyme
Trees: Almond; Apple; Cherry
Crystals: Amethyst; Coral; Emerald; Jade; Rose Quartz
Metal: Copper

Saturday
Influences: Animals; Bindings; New Beginnings; Official Matters; Overcoming Obstacles; Psychic Protection; Self-Control; Unfinished Business
Deities: Cronos; Horus; Saturn; The Fates
Archangel: Cassiel
Planet: Saturn
Element: Earth
Colors: Black; Grey; Indigo
Herbs/Incense: Myrrh ; Poppy Seeds;
Trees: Blackthorn; Cypress; Yew
Crystals: Hematite; Jet; Lodestone; Obsidian; Smokey Quartz
Metal: Lead; Pewter

Sunday

Influences: Agriculture; Ambition; Creativity; Increased Energy; Improving Health; Joy; Male Mysteries; Masculinity; New Projects; Power; Prosperity; Self-Confidence; Success; Victory
Deities: Apollo; Brigid; Helios; Llew; Lugh; Ra; Sol; Sunna
Archangel: Michael
Planet: Sun
Element: Fire
Colors: Gold; Orange; White; Yellow
Herbs/Incense: Chamomile; Cinnamon; Frankincense; Lemon; Marigold; Saffron; St. John's wort; Sunflower
Trees: Bay; Birch; Laurel
Crystals: Amber; Carnelian; Diamond; Quartz (clear); Tiger's Eye; Yellow Topaz
Metal: Gold

Solar Phases

General Solar Correspondences

Day: Sunday
Element: Fire
Archangel: Michael
Metal: Gold
Color: Gold, Orange, Yellow
Crystals: Amber, Carnelian, Diamond, Tiger's Eye, Topaz
Animals: Bear, Eagle, Hawk, Jaguar, Lion, Raven, Salmon, Stag
Trees: Bay, Birch, Laurel, Palm
Herbs/Incense: Chamomile, Cinnamon, Cloves, Frankincense, Olive, Rosemary, Saffron, St John's Wort

Dawn/Waxing

Related to the Spring Equinox and East, awakening energies, increasing light and energy, growth, new beginnings, new projects, courage, change, learning, studying, new skills, optimism, improving finances, and trust.

Midday
Related to the Summer Solstice and South, to high energy, potency, vitality, vigor, achievement, success, accomplishment, confidence, courage, power, love, fidelity, sexuality, commitment, resolution of legal matters, and intense healing or recovery from illness.

Waning/Dusk
Related to Autumn Equinox and West, letting go, releasing guilt or regrets, loss, bereavement, protection, age, wisdom, healing, home and family matters, gentle and mature love, justice, peace and acceptance.

Midnight
Related to the Winter Solstice and North, use for binding and banishing, revealing truth, forgiveness, endings that lead to new beginnings, rebirth, contacting absent family and friends, and communicating with spirit and ancestors.

Lunar Phases
General Lunar Correspondences:
Day: Monday
Element: Water
Archangel: Gabriel
Metal: Silver
Color: Silver, White
Crystals: Moonstone, Mother of Pearl, Opal, Pearl, Selenite
Animals: Bat, Heron, Moth, Owl, Snake, Wolf
Trees: Alder, Eucalyptus, Mimosa, Willow
Herbs/Incense: Coconut, Eucalyptus, Lemon, Lemon Balm, Lemon Verbena, Lotus, Jasmine, Mimosa, Myrrh, Poppy, Wintergreen

Dark

The three days when the moon is so close to the sun it is obscured from view and the sky appears dark. Related to the hidden aspects of ourselves, our shadow selves, occult knowledge, age, wisdom, balance and banishing. Associated with North, Samhain to Winter Solstice, and the Goddess as Crone. Not traditionally considered a time of magic workings, the dark moon is most often used as a time of introspection, reflection, meditation and letting go.

Deities: Crone; Cerridwen; Hecate
Herbs: Forget Me Not, Garlic, Parsley, Willow
Color: Black

New (First Glimpse of Waxing Moon) and Waxing

The new moon is the very first crescent of moon visible in the sky after the dark moon, sometimes referred to as Diana's Bow. The period between this first sighting and the night before the full moon is known as the waxing phase. Use the new moon for new beginnings and new projects, and the waxing phase for magic related to increase and growth. This phase is great for working towards a long-term goal, for improving health and wellbeing, for developing skills (especially psychic and intuitive skills) and enhancing fertility. Associated with East, Imbolc to Spring Equinox, and the Goddess as Maiden.

Deities: Maiden, Arianrhod, Artemis, Diana, Epona, Freyja, Rhiannon
Herbs: Aloe, Camphor, Lily, Mugwort, Poppy, White Rose
Color: White

Full

Most often celebrated as the three nights of Full Moon, although some paths only consider one night of Full Moon and other paths will celebrate for three days prior and three days after. The full moon is associated with the Goddess as Mother or Mistress, with

Beltaine to the Summer Solstice and with South. Considered the most powerful time for magic, the full moon is related to love, power, courage, justice, ambition, psychic awareness, female empowerment, healing, protection, and manifesting change.

Deities: Mother/Mistress, Aphrodite, Aradia, Danu, Gaia, Isis, Luna, Selene
Herbs: Dandelion, Frankincense, Marshmallow, Mugwort, Poppy
Color: Silver

Waning

The period after the full moon to the point of dark moon, related to decrease, endings, and banishing. Use the waning moon for removing obstacles, pain and illness; banishing harmful influences and destructive behaviors; ending relationships or projects; and dealing with grief and bereavement. Associated with the Goddess as Mother or Priestess, with Lughnassadh to the Autumn Equinox, and with West.

Deities: Mother/Priestess; Inanna; Ishtar; The Morrighan
Herbs: Garlic, Myrrh
Color: Grey

Color Correspondences

Amber

Symbolic of the Witch; Empowerment; Developing Skills; Building Self-Confidence

Direction: South; **Day:** Sunday; **Planet:** Sun; **Element:** Fire; **Chakra:** Solar Plexus; **Moon:** Waxing

Black

The Crone; Banishing; Binding; Confusion and Aggression; Death; Exorcism; Mourning; Night; Protection; Rebirth; Removing Discord; Transformation; Truth; Warding Negativity

Direction: North; **Day:** Saturday; **Planet:** Saturn; **Element:**

Water; **Chakra:** Base; **Moon:** Dark

Blue (Dark Blue)
The Goddess; Career; Change; Dreams; Internal Transformation;
Justice; Leadership Skills; Meditation; Protection; Water
Direction: West; **Day:** Thursday; **Planet:** Saturn and Jupiter;
Element: Water; **Chakra:** Throat; **Moon:** Waning

Blue (Light Blue)
Energetic Healing; Health and Well-Being; Intuition;
Opportunity; Patience; Peace; Psychic Awareness; Tranquility;
Direction: West; **Day:** Thursday; **Planet:** Saturn and Jupiter;
Element: Air; **Chakra:** Base; **Moon:** Waxing

Brown
Animal Health; Earth; Endurance; Home and Property; Physical;
Practicality; Reliability; Security; Stability; Tradition
Direction: North; **Day:** Saturday; **Planet:** Saturn; **Element:** Earth;
Chakra: Base; **Moon:** Dark

Copper
Business; Career; Conductivity; Finances; Professional Growth
Direction: South; **Day:** Wednesday; **Planet:** Mercury; **Element:**
Fire; **Chakra:** Sacral; **Moon:** Waxing

Gold
The God; Solar Deities; Achievement; Global Vision; Happiness;
Intense Healing; Longevity; Perfection; Physical Strength; Power;
Solar Magic; Success; Wealth
Direction: South; **Day:** Sunday; **Planet:** Sun; **Element:** Fire;
Chakra: Solar Plexus; **Moon:** Full

Grey
Adaptability; Compromise; Neutralizing; Obscuring; Otherworld

Travel; Peacekeeping; Protection; Repelling Psychic Attack; Secrets; Veiling; Vision Quests
Direction: East; **Day:** Wednesday; **Planet:** Mercury; **Element:** Air; **Chakra:** Base; **Moon:** Dark

Green
Lord and Lady of the Wildwood; The Green Man; Agriculture; Beauty; Commitment; Fertility; Fidelity; Growth; Harmony; Healing; Herblore; Horticulture; Love; Luck; Nature; Prosperity
Direction: North/West; **Day:** Friday; **Planet:** Venus; **Element:** Earth/Water; **Chakra:** Heart; **Moon:** Full

Orange
The God; Abundance; Action; Art; Balance; Confidence; Creativity; Fertility; Happiness; Independence; Inventiveness; Joy; Justice; Legal Matters; Music; Self-Esteem; Vitality
Direction: South; **Day:** Sunday; **Planet:** Sun; **Element:** Fire; **Chakra:** Solar Plexus; **Moon:** Waxing

Pink
Affection; Blessings; Children; Compassion; Family; Friendships; Gentle Bindings; Healing; Honor; Kindness; Love; Nurturing; Partnerships; Psychological Trauma; Reconciliations; Romance; Women's Mysteries
Direction: North; **Day:** Friday; **Planet:** Venus; **Element:** Earth; **Chakra:** Heart; **Moon:** Waxing

Purple
Ancient Wisdom; Counseling; Divination; Dreams; Elders; Intuition; Meditation; Peace; Psychic Power; Spiritual Knowledge; Teaching; Truth
Direction: East/West; **Day:** Thursday; **Planet:** Jupiter; **Element:** Air; **Chakra:** Brow; **Moon:** Full

Red

Action; Ambition; Assertiveness; Change; Competition; Courage; Determination; Enthusiasm; Love; Lust; Overcoming Odds; Passion; Pleasure; Power; Protection; Sensuality; Sexuality; Survival; Vigor; Vitality

Direction: South; **Day:** Tuesday; **Planet:** Mars; **Element:** Fire; **Chakra:** Base; **Moon:** Full

Silver

The Goddess; Lunar Deities; Astral Travel; Balance; Cycles; Clairvoyance; Intuition; Magic; Moon Magic; Mysticism; Psychic Abilities; Women's Mysteries

Direction: West/North; **Day:** Monday; **Planet:** Moon; **Element:** Water; **Chakra:** Crown; **Moon:** Full

White

Divinity; Easing Grief; Energy; Full Moon Magic; Intuition; Life-force; New Beginnings; Peace; Potential; Protection; Purification; Originality; Overcoming Depression and Exhaustion; Secrets; Spirit; Unity

Direction: Center; **Day:** Monday; **Planet:** Moon; **Element:** Water/Spirit; **Chakra:** Sacral/Crown; **Moon:** Full

Yellow

Adaptability; Clarity; Confidence; Communication; Creativity; Finances; Focus; Intellect; Learning; Logic; Memory; Mental Alertness; Repelling Envy and Malice; Technology; Versatility

Direction: East; **Day:** Wednesday; **Planet:** Mercury; **Element:** Air; **Chakra:** Solar Plexus; **Moon:** Waxing

Elemental Correspondences

Earth

Earth is our foundation, our nurturer and our great stabilizer. Use for any magic related to home, family and protection;

agriculture and horticulture; health and education; fertility and abundance; and any official matters or institutions involving law, politics, finance, health and education.

Direction: North

Solar Phase: Night

Lunar Phase: Dark

Planet: Venus, Saturn

Season: Winter

Energy: Receptive / Passive

Polarity: Feminine

Archangel: Uriel

Age: 60+

Colors: Black, Brown, Green

Tools: Pentacle, Cauldron

Animals: Antelope, Badger, Bear, Bee, Boar, Bull, Cow, Dog, Rabbit, Sheep, Snake, Spider, Stag, Wolf

Crystals: Agate (moss and tree), Amazonite, Aventurine, Emerald, Fossils, Hag Stones, Jet, Malachite, Rutilated Quartz, Smokey Quartz, Stromatolite, Tiger's Eye

Herbs: Bayberry, Blackthorn, Buckwheat, Clover, Cypress, Fir, Honeysuckle, Hollyhock, Patchouli, Pine, Primrose, Sage, Soapwort, Strawberry, Tansy, Vervain

Astrological Sign: Capricorn, Virgo, Taurus

Air

The winds of change herald new beginnings and bring information from far places. Use Air for any magic related to learning and study; for examinations, tests and mental challenges; for working with the sciences, technology or the media; for travel, moving home and changes in career or circumstances; for innovation, inspiration and new projects.

Direction: East

Solar Phase: Dawn

Lunar Phase: Waxing

Planet: Mercury, Jupiter, Uranus
Season: Spring
Energy: Active
Polarity: Masculine
Archangel: Raphael
Age: 0-20
Colors: White, Light Blue, Yellow
Tool: Wand or Sword / Athame
Animals: Birds of Prey, Butterflies, Dove, Eagle, Hawk, Nightingale, Winged Insects
Crystals: Amethyst, Angeline, Blue Lace Agate, Citrine, Clear Quartz, Herkimer Diamond, Lapis Lazuli, Sapphire, Sodalite, Sugilite, Turquoise
Herbs: Acacia, Almond, Anise, Benzoin, Bergamot, Cedar, Comfrey, Clary Sage, Dandelion, Dill, Dock, Fenugreek, Hazel, Lavender, Lemon Verbena, Marjoram, Mint, Mistletoe, Mulberry, Nutmeg, Parsley, Sandalwood, Sage, Wormwood
Astrological Sign: Aquarius, Libra, Gemini

Fire

Fire the great transformer, the lover, the leader and the warrior. Use Fire in magic related to wise power and leadership skills; for any creative or artistic projects; for courage, competition and success; for love, sex, passion and pleasure; for protection (especially in direct attacks), binding and banishing; and for transformation and manifestation.

Direction: South
Solar Phase: Midday
Lunar Phase: Full
Planet: Sun, Mars
Season: Summer
Energy: Projective / Active
Polarity: Masculine
Archangel: Michael

Age: 20-40
Colors: Gold, Orange, Red, Yellow
Tool: Wand or Sword / Athame
Animals: Cat, Dragon, Dragonfly, Firefly, Lion, Stag
Crystals: Amber, Bloodstone, Boji Stone, Carnelian, Garnet, Lava, Sunstone, Obsidian, Ruby
Herbs: Angelica, Asafoetida, Ash, Basil, Bay, Cedar, Cinnamon, Cinquefoil, Clove, Coriander, Dill, Dragon's Blood, Fennel, Frankincense, Garlic, Holly, Horsechestnut, Hyssop, Juniper, Lily of the Valley, Madder, Mandrake, Mustard, Nettle, Oak, Olive, Peony, Rosemary, Rue, Saffron, Sunflower, Tarragon
Astrological Sign: Aries, Leo, Sagittarius

Water
Life-giving Water, the beginning and the end. Use Water in magic related to love, relationships, and friendship; for dreams, scrying, divination and any moon magic; for gentle endings and releasing that which no longer serves us; for healing, cleansing and purification; for dealing with grief and bereavement; for women's mysteries and for connecting with the Divine, with the Universe and with all people.
Direction: West
Solar Phase: Dusk
Lunar Phase: Waning
Planet: Neptune, Moon, Pluto
Season: Autumn
Energy: Receptive / Passive
Polarity: Feminine
Archangel: Gabriel
Age: 40-60
Colors: Dark Blue, Purple, Silver, Turquoise
Tool: Chalice
Animals: Alligator, Beaver, Crab, Crocodile, Dolphin, Duck, Frog, Heron, Otter, Salmon, Seahorse, Seal, Starfish, Swan,

Whale

Crystals: Aquamarine, Calcite, Coral, Fluorite, Jade, Moonstone, Opal, Pearl, Tourmaline

Herbs: Alder, Aloe, Apple, Ash, Balm Gilead, Belladonna, Bindweed, Birch, Burdock, Camphor, Cardamom, Catnip, Chamomile, Coltsfoot, Daisy, Dog Rose, Feverfew, Foxglove, Geranium, Hellebore, Hemlock, Hemp, Henbane, Ivy, Jasmine, Lily, Lady's Mantle, Marshmallow, Meadowsweet, Mugwort, Myrrh, Myrtle, Periwinkle, Poppy, Rose, Rowan, Scullcap, Snowdrop, Thyme, Violet, Yew

Astrological Sign: Pisces, Cancer, Scorpio

Sabbat Correspondences

Samhain

Breaking bread with the dead, Samhain is the last harvest, the end of the Celtic summer and the day to honor our beloved dead. A festival of physical and psychic protection, divination and prophecy; facing fears, exploring our shadow selves and embracing the dark aspects of our life; honoring the elders in our community, caring for the sick or terminally ill and remembering those passed over; dealing with death, grief and bereavement; exploring the darker side of our sexuality and facing any issues that affect our sexual relationships; reaping the last harvest, preparing for a time of introspection, and letting go of all that no longer serves us.

Keyword: Transition

Element: Water / Earth

Direction: North-West

Energy: Waning

Solar Phase: Dusk to Midnight

Lunar Phase: Waning Crescent to Dark

Herbs: Alder, Apple, Aspen, Belladonna, Blackthorn, Catnip, Cypress, Elder, Hellebore, Hemlock, Henbane, Honeysuckle, Juniper, Mullein, Myrrh, Parsley, Pumpkin, Rowan, Thistle,

Valerian, Wormwood, Yew

Yule / Winter Solstice
Do not dismay, for the Sun is born upon this day. The Winter Solstice brings the promise of rebirth, the hope of new life and new light, during the hardest and coldest part of the year. This is a festival of hope, patience and acceptance; a time of family and friends, sharing, giving and receiving; a celebration of all domestic aspects, home and property, happiness, stability and financial security; and for rituals of regeneration, renewal, rebirth and restoration.
Keyword: Rebirth
Element: Fire / Air
Direction: North
Energy: Rising / Waxing
Solar Phase: Midnight
Lunar Phase: Dark to New
Herbs: Apple, Ash, Bayberry, Blackthorn, Calendula, Cinnamon, Cypress, Frankincense, Holly, Ivy, Juniper, Mistletoe, Oak, Violet

Imbolc
In the belly of the earth, life now stirs. This festival revolves around the promise of spring; a transition festival of life and light within the cold hand of winter. A new beginning, a form of regeneration and regrowth, a chance to melt away old patterns and behaviors, a chance to heal, and an opportunity to nurture new life, babies, young children and animals.
Keyword: Trust
Element: Fire / Earth
Direction: North-East
Energy: Rising / Waxing
Solar Phase: Midnight to Dawn
Lunar Phase: Waxing Crescent
Herbs: Alder, Benzoin, Birch, Elm, Heather, Lily of the Valley,

Periwinkle, Rowan, Snowdrop, Tansy, Willow, Wormwood

Ostara / Spring Equinox
Spring cometh and light takes hold. This festival celebrates spring, the tipping point where light overcomes darkness, and the visible growth and fertility of the land. A festival of bold new beginnings and opportunities; of new love, fertility, growth, conception, and pregnancy; of creative ventures, new projects, and travel; of positive life changes, spring cleaning and ridding ourselves of that which no longer serves us.
Keyword: Beginnings
Element: Air
Direction: East
Energy: Balanced, but waxing
Solar Phase: Dawn
Lunar Phase: Waxing Quarter
Herbs: Alder, Apple, Ash, Benzoin, Birch, Bluebell, Calendula, Caraway, Coltsfoot, Daisy, Forget Me Not, Frankincense, Gorse, Lemon Verbena, Mugwort, Nettle, Pine, Tansy, Violet

Beltaine
The Bel-Fires burn and the fertile fields and forests are home to new love and laughter. Beltaine is the beginning of the Celtic summer, and is marked by the modern May Day festivals. A celebration of all forms of fertility, physical, emotional, spiritual and all new projects, careers, business and finance. A festival of love, consummation, commitment, and abundance; generosity and giving; creativity and inspiration; and strength of belief.
Keyword: Fertility
Element: Fire / Earth
Direction: South-East
Energy: Waxing / Increasing
Solar Phase: Dawn to Midday
Lunar Phase: Gibbous

Herbs: Apple, Belladonna, Birch, Cinquefoil, Clover, Daisy, Dandelion, Dill, Dog Rose, Elder, Hawthorn, Honeysuckle, Horsechestnut, Lily of the Valley, Mallow, Oak, Primrose, Rose, Willow, Woodruff

Litha / Summer Solstice

The height of power is a tipping point, an increase leading to an inevitable decreasing spiral. This is a festival of joy, abundance, strength, energy, self-confidence, health, wealth, fertility and male potency. A time to seize new chances, enjoy the present, maximize opportunities, celebrate success and resolve seemingly overwhelming problems.

Keyword: Power
Element: Fire
Direction: South
Energy: Peak, tipping into waning
Solar Phase: Midday
Lunar Phase: Full
Herbs: Angelica, Apple, Ash, Bay, Calendula, Chamomile, Daisy, Dill, Dog Rose, Elder, Fennel, Fern, Feverfew, Heather, Honeysuckle, Lavender, Marjoram, Mistletoe, Oak, St. John's Wort, Strawberry, Violet, Yarrow

Lughnassadh

In love of the Goddess and all her people, the God casts his strength into the fields of grain, and prepares to journey towards death and be reborn again. Lughnassadh is a time of abundance and plenty, but even within this time of light and joy the touch of darkness is felt. A celebration of harvest, commitment and sacrifice; justice, freedom and leadership; generosity and giving; reaping the rewards of projects, careers and commitments; fighting against inequality and injustice; protecting the innocent; and stabilizing the home environment in preparation of winter.

Keyword: Sacrifice
Element: Earth

Direction: South-West
Energy: Waning
Solar Phase: Midday to Dusk
Lunar Phase: Disseminating
Herbs: Alder, Apple, Basil, Benzoin, Borage, Chicory, Daisy, Fennel, Fenugreek, Frankincense, Gorse, Honeysuckle, Ivy, Marshmallow, Mugwort, Nasturtium, Oak, Pine, Poppy, Sunflower, Vine

Mabon / Autumn Equinox

In balance we begin our great descent, the doors to the underworld open and the dying and rising Gods travel into the tomb and womb of the Great Mother. The Autumn Equinox is the great harvest time, a time of abundance and reaping all we have sown. Light and dark are in balance, but darkness takes hold. A festival to honor relationships, family and friendship; to celebrate the completion of tasks and goals; for mending quarrels and troubled relationships; for forgiving ourselves; for preparing for the future; for preparing for death and transitions; and for any rituals related to food, shelter and resources for vulnerable communities.

Keyword: Balance
Element: Water
Direction: West
Energy: Balanced, but waning
Solar Phase: Dusk
Lunar Phase: Waning Quarter
Herbs: Acorn, Alder, Apple, Ash, Basil, Benzoin, Blackberry, Buckwheat, Calendula, Cedar, Chicory, Corn, Cornflower, Cypress, Daisy, Dog Rose, Elder, Frankincense, Hawthorn, Hazel, Ivy, Myrrh, Parsley, Poppy, Rose, Yew

Planetary Associations

Jupiter

The Sky Father, astrologically representing the expression of the personality in the wider context of society and culture. Use Jupiter for all forms of increase and expansion, extending one's influence into the world, authority, career, conscious wisdom, creativity, fidelity, justice, law, loyalty, marriage, permanent relationships (personal and professional).

Mars

The Red Planet, astrologically represents initiative, independence, and distance from others. Use Mars for change, courage, independence and taking the initiative. Mars is a strong passionate planet and can also be used for strength and vitality, defeating opposition, overcoming odds, and any acts of passion and wild love.

Mercury

Mercury the Messenger astrologically represents the method in which the basic character is communicated and expressed in the world. Use Mars for adaptability and versatility, clear communication, learning, studying, mastering new skills and technology, examinations and tests, and travel. Can also be used for uncovering and repelling envy, malice and deceit.

Moon

Lady Luna astrologically represents the emotional and subconscious aspects of the personality. Use the Moon for all family and home matters, gardening, healing, for women, children and childbirth. The ebb and flow of the Moon relates to the sea, fertility, emotions and the human psyche. Can also be used for aiding spiritual development, psychic awareness, clairvoyance, visionary dreaming.

Saturn

The Ringed Planet, astrologically represents the expression of personality and an individual's interactions within societal restrictions. Use Saturn for resolving any unfinished business, slow moving matters, and any long-standing obstacles. Can also be used for endings that lead to new beginnings, regaining self-control, banishing pain and illness, and accepting circumstances, limitations and situations that cannot be changed.

Sun

The Divine Sun astrologically represents the essential self, identity, and unique qualities. Use the Sun for all forms of potent and high energy, for joy, health, prosperity, positivity, self-confidence, and innovation. The Sun relates to all matters concerning fathers, and can also be used to break a run of bad luck.

Venus

The Evening Star, astrologically represents the partnerships and interactions between significant others, parents, lovers, families, friends and close business partners. Use Venus in all forms of art and creativity, beauty, love, relationships, friendships, sexuality and sensuality. Can also be used for environmental matters, horticulture, fertility and women's mysteries.

Planetary Hours

Planetary hours change dependent upon the sunrise and sunset on any given day within the year, and the "hours" will not be exactly an hour long. To work them out, first find out the times of sunrise and sunset. Calculate the total minutes in the day between the sunrise and the sunset, and divide the total minutes by twelve to reveal the length of your daylight hours. Repeat this exercise for the minutes between sunset and sunrise to calculate the length of your planetary hours in the night.

Planetary Hours

Sunrise to Sunset Chart

Hour	Sunday	Monday	Tuesday	Wednesday	Thursday	Friday	Saturday
1	Sun	Moon	Mars	Mercury	Jupiter	Venus	Saturn
2	Venus	Saturn	Sun	Moon	Mars	Mercury	Jupiter
3	Mercury	Jupiter	Venus	Saturn	Sun	Moon	Mars
4	Moon	Mars	Mercury	Jupiter	Venus	Saturn	Sun
5	Saturn	Sun	Moon	Mars	Mercury	Jupiter	Venus
6	Jupiter	Venus	Saturn	Sun	Moon	Mars	Mercury
7	Mars	Mercury	Jupiter	Venus	Saturn	Sun	Moon
8	Sun	Moon	Mars	Mercury	Jupiter	Venus	Saturn
9	Venus	Saturn	Sun	Moon	Mars	Mercury	Jupiter
10	Mercury	Jupiter	Venus	Saturn	Sun	Moon	Mars
11	Moon	Mars	Mercury	Jupiter	Venus	Saturn	Sun
12	Saturn	Sun	Moon	Mars	Mercury	Jupiter	Venus

Sunset to Sunrise Chart

Hour	Sunday	Monday	Tuesday	Wednesday	Thursday	Friday	Saturday
1	Jupiter	Venus	Saturn	Sun	Moon	Mars	Mercury
2	Mars	Mercury	Jupiter	Venus	Saturn	Sun	Moon
3	Sun	Moon	Mars	Mercury	Jupiter	Venus	Saturn
4	Venus	Saturn	Sun	Moon	Mars	Mercury	Jupiter
5	Mercury	Jupiter	Venus	Saturn	Sun	Moon	Mars
6	Moon	Mars	Mercury	Jupiter	Venus	Saturn	Sun
7	Saturn	Sun	Moon	Mars	Mercury	Jupiter	Venus
8	Jupiter	Venus	Saturn	Sun	Moon	Mars	Mercury
9	Mars	Mercury	Jupiter	Venus	Saturn	Sun	Moon
10	Sun	Moon	Mars	Mercury	Jupiter	Venus	Saturn
11	Venus	Saturn	Sun	Moon	Mars	Mercury	Jupiter
12	Mercury	Jupiter	Venus	Saturn	Sun	Moon	Mars

About Romany

Romany Rivers is a British-born artist, poet, and Pagan author. As a Priestess and co-founder of Moon River Wicca in England, Romany often uses poetry and modern interpretations of fairy-tales to create unique celebrations, festivals, and rituals. Aside from her work as a Priestess and artist, she is also well known for her work in the holistic health community as a Reiki Master and Tarot reader. Romany now resides in Nova Scotia, Canada, pursuing dreams of a sustainable, family-focused and rural lifestyle whilst providing holistic and family support services to the community.

Other Titles by Romany Rivers

Poison Pen Letters to Myself
Poison Pen Letters to Myself chronicles a very personal journey through the years overcoming severe bouts of depression and consequently creating a more holistic and spiritual lifestyle. The chapters Red Letters, Return to Sender and Addressee Unknown reveal periods of depression and anxiety; anger and healing; and acceptance and spiritual growth. The words in these pages were not written for mass consumption. They were not artfully crafted for reading aloud in dim rooms to a soundtrack of clicking fingers and Parisian style applause. They were not intended as political statements or a way of reaching other wayward wandering souls. Over the last two decades they were poured, purged, scribbled and spat onto scraps of paper, napkins, backs of hands, into empty pages and blank spaces of other books. At times of sorrow, frustration, confusion, acceptance and joy these words made sense of the minds muddled meanderings. Within these pages you will find heart-breaking, heart-healing honesty that crosses the divide and touches the souls of others.

Moon Books invites you to begin or deepen your encounter with
Paganism, in all its rich, creative, flourishing forms.